What People Are Saying...
about the Messianic Daily Devotional

"How absolutely wonderful!!! Kevin tells us not to forget the Scriptures, and consider ways to extend your devotional time. Well, that is what happened for me. I found myself using what I had read to dig even deeper into the Scriptures. My focus for the day changed—what a Blessing!! You can actually feel the renewing of your mind taking place. I was constantly being drawn back, throughout the day, to what I had read and studied that morning. What freedom!!!! Thank you, Kevin!!! Blessings to you." -T.A.

"I love this book! It is not just an inspiration, but it also encourages a person. It is a book that teaches what many others do not: the fact that our focus should always be on the Almighty... This is a wonderful book which I would like to see everyone have in their hands. [The] devotional messages... are so uplifting and encouraging that even my husband, who is a non-believer, is reading them as well.... Keep up the good work that you have been chosen to do, for it is truly excellent." -F.C.

"I just received [the book] and I am enjoying it immensely. It offers encouragement as well as challenges me to live a life daily devoted to Elohim. It speaks to the desires of my heart and spirit in a way that no other devotional ever has. I would highly recommend it to anyone [who] wants to grow in their faith. Thank you, Kevin, for an excellent book.... May Elohim continue to pour out His blessings and love on you and your family and this ministry." -M.A.

"From the first page, we knew that there was something different about this devotional. It does not contain just nice thoughts, but reaches down into the very depths of your being asking you to "come up here" to a new level of commitment. We will continue to share this devotional with others. Thank you!"
-D.F. & C.F.

"This is the first devotional I have read that really challenges me to critically look at my attitudes and behaviors and to humbly ask forgiveness from our gracious Lord where I have sinned and fallen short. Thank you for having the courage to speak and write what ADONAI would have you say." -K.B.

"I read the devotional every morning, and have been so blessed. It seems to be just what I need for that day. I love the richness of the [Messianic Jewish] insight. I ordered 10 copies and gave them to my friends." -C.T.

"I cannot begin to tell you what a blessing this is. I now have a deeper and more intimate walk with Yeshua, as I have prayed long and hard for a Messianic Devotional. This is absolutely perfect. I pray that our Father will bless Mr. Geoffrey to do more because they truly make you think. Let's just say that you cannot afford to be without one. [It] would make an awesome gift for someone you really care about and love." -C.L.

MESSIANIC

Mo'adiym

DEVOTIONAL

KEVIN GEOFFREY

PERFECT *Word*

P · U · B · L · I · S · H · I · N · G

A ministry of Perfect Word Ministries

A *ministry of Perfect Word Ministries*

PO Box 82954 • Phoenix, AZ 85071
www.PerfectWordMinistries.com
1-888-321-PWMI

All Scriptures from *Young's Literal Translation of the Holy Bible
(1862/1898) by J.N. Young,* which is in the public domain. Our
updating and re-rendering of the text for the modern Messianic
reader is ©2007 by Perfect Word Ministries, Inc.

ISBN #: 0-9785504-1-2

Printed in the United States of America

וַיְדַבֵּר יהוה אֶל־מֹשֶׁה לֵּאמֹר
דַּבֵּר אֶל־בְּנֵי יִשְׂרָאֵל וְאָמַרְתָּ אֲלֵהֶם מוֹעֲדֵי יהוה
אֲשֶׁר־תִּקְרְאוּ אֹתָם מִקְרָאֵי קֹדֶשׁ אֵלֶּה הֵם מוֹעֲדָי

*"And ADONAI spoke to Moshe, saying, 'Speak to
the sons of Yis'rael, and you will say to them,
"These are [the] appointed times of ADONAI,
which you [are to] proclaim; holy convocations.
They are My appointed times…"'"*

וַיִּקְרָא *Vayik'ra (Leviticus) 23:1-2*

Table of Contents

Preface

When the decision was made to begin publishing a series of Messianic Jewish daily devotional books, I was extremely excited. I felt confident that they would not only be well-received, but that they would also meet a great *need* in the Body of Messiah. Even now, my heart-cry is to see believers from all walks of life develop the life-changing daily discipline of devotion, so that *together* we can get down to the business of being useful, dedicated, effective, *"sold-out"* disciples of Messiah.

But as we were developing the ideas for this series, I think it was the prospect of producing a volume of devotionals *specifically* for ADONAI's appointed times that really sealed the deal for me. In all the devotional books that I have seen, the topics are somewhat random. Even in an annual devotional where every day of the year is accounted for, there's really no connection between the subject matter of the devotional and the actual day on which it is intended to be read.

Not so for the *Messianic Mo'adiym Devotional*!

The premise of this book is simple: ADONAI has made very specific appointments for Israel to keep and honor for the sake of remembering who He is, staying focused on Him, and knowing Him more. A tool such as the *Messianic Mo'adiym Devotional* will not only help us to *keep* these appointments when they are scheduled, but will *prepare* us to enter into their fullness as disciples of Messiah.

To me, this is the essence of discipleship—to be with the Master where He is, to follow Him and do as He instructs, and then to reap the benefits and insights *in the doing...* to allow the humble act of *following* to remake us in the image of our Master, so that we can fulfill our hearts' desire to be like Him.

When we keep ADONAI's *Mo'adiym*, we receive their inherent instruction. Each appointed time has a very specific point to teach us about our Father, our people, our purpose on this earth, and our relationship with the Master—the Messiah Yeshua. It's a teaching we can't learn by reading or hearing... it's learned by *doing*—"doing" according to the Scriptures, and not according to the innovations or imaginations of men. The *Messianic Mo'adiym Devotional* is designed to *facilitate* that "doing" by directing us to the truth of the Scriptures, and then preparing our hearts and minds for the *exact moment in time* that the Father has already ordained.

Thank you for allowing me to walk with you during each of ADONAI's annual appointed times as we continue to follow in the footsteps of our Master. As you make this book part of your daily devotions to God, I pray that the Scriptures contained herein will captivate and draw you; that their corresponding devotional writings will spark in you a fresh understanding of the Scriptures; and that as you begin to pray in accordance with the Word of God, the Spirit will lead you into a time of deep and meaningful devotion, worship and praise that will change your life—today, forever, and for good.

In Yeshua,

Kevin Geoffrey
March 1, 2007

Introduction

The *Messianic Mo'adiym Devotional* is the first of several planned companion volumes to the immensely well-received *Messianic Daily Devotional*, published in 2006. Continuing in the tradition of its predecessor, the *Messianic Mo'adiym Devotional* offers insightful, challenging, Scripture-based devotional writings with a unique, but distinctly Messianic Jewish point of view.

It is important to note that our devotionals are not designed to be resources for learning about Messianic Jewish theology. The source matter for this *particular* book did occasionally warrant some explanation within the devotionals themselves, as well as an additional appendix containing basic teachings about the *Mo'adiym* (appointed times). As much as possible, however, we purposely avoided a teaching style intended to impart *information*, and instead opted for a personal style designed to encourage *devotion*. Time and again, this approach has been affirmed by our readers, as they consistently comment that these devotionals are like none they have ever read before.

Unlike the *Messianic Daily Devotional*—which covers many different topics related to our daily walk with Messiah—the *Messianic Mo'adiym Devotional* has a very specific focus: Israel's annual feasts, fasts and appointed times. Each devotional writing is therefore intended to be read on a very specific day of Israel's calendar in order to enhance and deepen the practical and spiritual significance of each *moed*.

Since this book's readership will undoubtedly have many varying backgrounds and levels of experience with the *Mo'adiym*, we felt it was essential to include introductory teaching material to supplement the devotional writings. Not only do we want you, the reader, to know what the Scriptures teach about the *Mo'adiym* in general, but we also believe it is important for you to understand *our* perspective of them, so that you can get the most out of each devotional.

To that end—whether you have been observing the *Mo'adiym* all your life, or have no experience with ADONAI's appointed times whatsoever—**we strongly encourage you to read the appendix, beginning on p. 143, before you begin the devotionals.** Though the information provided is by no means exhaustive, we hope it will serve to set the proper tone for the book, allowing you to enter into the fullness of all that ADONAI has for you during His designated seasons this year.

Features

All of the devotionals in this book begin with a passage of Scripture, upon which the devotional writing is based. These are not teachings or commentaries on the passage, but are exhortative writings that are intended to encourage discipleship and devotion to God. Each devotional concludes with a suggested prayer that will help give you a "jump-start" as you enter into a time of fellowship with ADONAI.

Most of the devotionals contain "restored" Hebrew names and places, the most obvious of which are Yeshua (rendered in most English translations of the Bible as "Jesus"), and Messiah (rendered in most English translations as "Christ"). This "restoration" was done for several reasons. First, it serves as a reminder of the Hebraic nature of our Scriptures—and how often they can be truly foreign to our western-thinking minds. Second, it demonstrates the ongoing and perpetual Jewishness of our faith and our Messiah. Finally, it helps to increase our familiarity with and love for the Hebrew language—the native tongue of the nation of Israel, and of her promised redeemer, Yeshua.

Not wishing to trivialize the use of Hebrew within a book written for an English-speaking audience, we have gone a step beyond simply embedding *transliterated*[1] Hebrew. In passages of Scripture that were originally written in Hebrew, we have also included the actual Hebrew letters with their *nikudot* (vowel marks or vowel points).[2] This should be especially beneficial for those who are just beginning to learn the Hebrew language. In some cases, we have included the *translated*[3] English word just after the restored Hebrew and transliteration. However, a reverse glossary—alphabetized according to the transliterated English—is also provided at the back of the book, enabling the reader to look up the meaning of each Hebrew word used in the devotionals.

The Sacred Name

For the sake of brevity, there are two familiar Hebrew words used throughout the devotionals that are rendered with transliteration *alone*—Yeshua and Adonai.[4] However, when the word "ADONAI" is printed

---

[1] A transliteration is a phonetic representation of words from another language. For instance, "Yeshua" is an English transliteration of the Hebrew, יֵשׁוּעַ.
[2] Most of the vowel sounds in Hebrew are not represented by letters of the *alef-beit*, but instead have been preserved for posterity through the vowel-pointing system of the *nikudot*.
[3] A translation gives the *meaning* of a word, while transliteration gives only its *pronunciation*.
[4] A title for God, meaning Lord or Master.

with all capital letters, it actually represents a *different* word altogether: יהוה, the "Sacred Name" of God.[5]

So why don't we use an English transliteration to help us pronounce the Sacred Name? The reason is that we simply do not know how to properly pronounce it. According to Jewish tradition, the Name is not to be spoken aloud, out of proper respect for the Holy One. Whenever the Scriptures were read aloud, the reader would speak "Adonai," rather than uttering the Name itself. Thus, when the Jewish scribes were adding the *nikudot* to the Scriptures, they purposely superimposed the *nikudot* for אֲדֹנָי, *Adonai* upon the Name in order to remind the reader to make the appropriate substitution. With time, the pronunciation of the Name was lost—or at least obscured beyond recovery.

Though some scholars and others individuals maintain that the pronunciation of the Name has indeed been preserved from antiquity—or can be reasonably discerned from what we know of Hebrew— it is *our* belief that this is just not so. Therefore, with no confidence in the accuracy of any given pronunciation, we have opted to represent יהוה with "ADONAI," in keeping with the tradition. Where יהוה appears next to אֲדֹנָי, *Adonai* in the text, the name that is rendered with capital letters is the one used to represent the Sacred Name, i.e. *Adonai 'ELOHIYM*.[6]

---

[5] In English, this name is sometimes represented as YHWH or YHVH, the English letters which correspond to the four Hebrew letters of The Name.

[6] The Hebrew, אֱלֹהִים, *'Elohiym*, and occasionally אֵל, *El*, is usually translated in English as "God." Where you see the word "God" in the devotional Scripture passages originally written in Hebrew, it is translating this word.

Young's Literal Translation of the Holy Bible (1862/1898) by J.N. Young

One of the challenges in devotional writing—or any kind of Bible teaching, for that matter—is avoiding personal "inspiration" or "revelation" sparked solely from the English translation. When a teacher relies exclusively on a specific translation, he risks having a distorted view of the text, or even missing its point altogether.

Although translators do their best to retain the meanings of the original text, there is always some linguistic work and paraphrasing based on the translator's understanding. While some Bible translations take more liberty than others, their goal is generally to make the Scriptures more readable for the new audience—and a translation that is more readable is therefore more meaningful. While this approach is helpful in communicating ideas and concepts, such alterations unavoidably add to or change the meaning of a passage when it is read subjectively.

In an attempt to compensate for the skewed "inspiration" that can come from reading English translations, we chose to work with the *Young's Literal Translation*. First published in 1862, this "literal" translation attempts to retain direct one-to-one word translations, word order, colloquialisms, and literal phrase renderings from the original language. As you can imagine, this makes for a sometimes dramatically different reading from other English translations. Despite this advantage, however, the "old English" style of the text is often cumbersome, making it very difficult to use at times.

Thankfully, another aspect of the *Young's* worked in our favor—the translation is in the public domain, and therefore free from copyright. As such, we had the freedom to work with the text, bringing the language into 21st century North American English. We were also able to restore the Hebrew names of people and places, along with other words which we felt worked better in the original language. As we made these updates, we were constantly forced to go back to the original languages, as well as making comparisons with various other English translations. In the end, we arrived at a fresh, meaningful, and hopefully accurate translation.

Although every attempt was made to keep the translation as literal as possible, there were some instances where additional English words were necessary. Where Young added words not in the original language, they are set off from the italicized Scriptures as normal text. Where *we* added words that were neither in the Young's nor in the original text, they are set off by brackets. These words were added to make for a smooth, unencumbered reading of the passage—but in most cases, you will find that they can be read and understood without our bracketed embellishments.

The Daily Discipline of Devotion

Each of us is in a different stage of life, with varying responsibilities, pressures, and other demands on our time and energy. As disciples of Messiah, however, we cannot afford to allow *life* to dictate how we *live*. The only way we can ever hope to gain control over our lives is to yield ourselves completely to God. Though we may prefer it to be otherwise, such surrender is not a one-time event—it is ongoing, and requires a daily commitment. Undying devotion to God is key to living an effective, useful, *and happy* life for Messiah.

One way to begin developing that daily discipline of devotion is through the use of devotional resources such as the *Messianic Daily Devotional* and the *Messianic Mo'adiym Devotional*. Though you may find the writings to be inspirational and useful for sharpening you as a believer in Yeshua, these books are only intended to be a starting place for what we pray will be a meaningful and ever-deepening devotional life.

The following are just a few practical suggestions for how to incorporate the *Messianic Mo'adiym Devotional* into your life, as you continually develop that daily discipline of devotion.

Examples of Ways to Use the Devotional Book

- ❖ In private devotions—to grow in your relationship with ADONAI as you meet with Him at His appointed times

- ❖ During family devotions—to begin a time of prayer, discussion, or study

- ❖ As a discipleship tool—to help new believers get into the Word and allow ADONAI to transform their lives

- ❖ Between accountability partners—to read together or apart, in order to discuss or share insights that will strengthen you both as disciples of Messiah

Goals to Consider for Your Mo'adiym Devotions

- ❖ Set aside a special time on each *moed* to be alone with God—congregational meetings are wonderful, but they should never take the place of our personal time with Him.

- ❖ Read a devotional on each *moed*, but don't forget the Scriptures! Remember, each devotional Scripture passage is but a small fragment of a larger book and chapter.

- ❖ Pray! Rather than *concluding* your devotional time with the prayers we have provided, use them to jump-start your time with ADONAI.

- ❖ Consider ways to extend your devotional time— for example, put on your favorite praise and worship CD and see what happens!

This is *devotion*: to devote ourselves fully to our God, to give our lives over to Him completely, and to be captivated by the gravity and grace of His presence, so that *"in Him, we [will] live, and move, and be…"*[7]

---

[7] Acts 17:28

MESSIANIC
Mo'adiym
DEVOTIONAL

It Is a Sacrifice

"You are to observe this thing, for [it is] a statute to you and to your sons—to the age. And it will be, when you come in to the land which ADONAI gives you, as He has spoken, that you keep this עֲבֹדָה, 'avodah (service). And it will come to pass when your sons say to you, 'What is this עֲבֹדָה, 'avodah you have?' that you will say, 'It is a sacrifice of פֶּסַח, Pesach to ADONAI, who passed over the houses of the sons of יִשְׂרָאֵל, Yis'rael in מִצְרַיִם, Mitz'rayim (Egypt), in His smiting the מִצְרַיִם, Mitz'rayim, and our houses He delivered.' And the people bowed [down] and worshipped."
שְׁמוֹת *Sh'mot (Exodus) 12:24-28*

Tonight will be different from all other nights. It will be a night of celebration, of deliverance, of freedom, of salvation. We will remember what ADONAI did for us so long ago—how in that one night, he changed our lives forever. We will remember His glory, His power, and His redemption. We will remember how, by the shedding of innocent blood, we were set free. Tonight, we will recall how ADONAI saved Yis'rael—and all of us—once and for all.

The annual sacrifice of Pesach commemorates the night that the nation was reborn—this is the service that all Yis'rael is commanded to keep each year forever. Oppressed and enslaved, Yis'rael cried out, not knowing if anyone would respond. But ADONAI, the God of Yis'rael, heard their cries and answered with wondrous signs—and with a Deliverer. This night was the end of Yis'rael's oppression and slavery—this is the night that ADONAI smote Yis'rael's oppressors, *"and our houses He delivered."*

Yis'rael was set free as a new nation, but her salvation was only the beginning. That night, Yis'rael was released to begin her true journey—one that would finally lead her home. Her deliverance had come, but the path that ADONAI had laid before her was still ahead. How she traveled that road would determine how she would live the rest of her life. Would she follow ADONAI's commands and inherit the promises to Av'raham, or would she quickly go astray and wander from ADONAI's promises and His peace?

In the Pesach, we too are reborn. Oppressed by and enslaved to sin, we too cried out, not knowing if anyone would respond. But ADONAI, the God of Yis'rael, heard our cries and answered with wondrous signs—and by the shedding of the innocent blood of our Deliverer, the Messiah Yeshua, *"the Lamb of God who is taking away the sin of the world." (Yochanan 1:29)* Tonight, we are new again, set free… but our salvation is only the beginning. How will we walk the path that ADONAI has laid before us? Will we wander astray and squander our salvation, or will we follow ADONAI's commands and walk in the ways of the Master? What is this *'avodah* we have? It is a sacrifice of Pesach to ADONAI…

તે છે

ADONAI, God of Yis'rael, thank You for setting Your people free! I praise You, O God—Redeemer, Savior, Deliverer. I bless Your Name, for I am new again in You. Thank You, Father, for the Pesach sacrifice of Your Son, by whose blood I am "passed over." Now help me never to wander, but to follow Your commands as I walk the path You have laid before me….

You Are Unleavened

> *"Clean out, therefore, the old leaven, that you may be a new batch [of dough], because you are unleavened, for our* פֶּסַח*, Pesach—* מָשִׁיחַ*, Mashiyach (Messiah)— also was sacrificed for us, so that we may keep the Feast not with old leaven, nor with the leaven of evil and wickedness, but with [the]* מַצָּה*, matzah of purity and truth." 1Corinthians 5:7-8*

The Feast of Matzah (Unleavened Bread) speaks of who we truly are in Messiah: redeemed and delivered from a life of sin. We now have two identities from which to choose—the old one, and the new. Before Messiah saved us, we had only one choice—*"evil and wickedness."* But now that He has set us free from sin, there is an alternative—*"purity and truth."* The reason we struggle with our flesh is because we fail to remember that *in reality*, we are now *unleavened*.

Yeshua, our Passover lamb, has been sacrificed once and for all. Because of that sacrifice, our debt has been paid, and we no longer owe our lives to the grave. Just as the blood of the first Pesach sacrifices was applied to the doorposts of the homes of the children of Israel while they were held captive in Egypt, so has Yeshua's blood been applied to the doorposts of our hearts, and ADONAI's judgment has passed over us. We are now free to leave our leaven behind in Egypt and start a new journey without the old yeast of our lives.

Leaven is symbolic of sin because it is *insidious*. *"A little yeast leavens the whole batch" (vs. 6)*—it spreads like a disease and thoroughly permeates the dough. When we entertain sin at even the most minute level, it creeps in *and multiplies*—it spreads, taking over our minds and bodies one little piece at a time.

This is the crime for many believers in Yeshua—we allow and entertain sin in our lives when *in reality*, we are no longer sinners. When we partake of the matzah, it reminds us not only that *"our Pesach—Messiah—also was sacrificed for us,"* but that He has been sacrificed so that our reality could be *unleavened*. This is who we truly are: righteous, and without sin. When we sin, giving in to the desires of our flesh, we remember far too well who we used to be.

So here is the challenge: which voice will we believe? The one telling us that even though we are saved, in reality we're still just sinners; or the one telling us that we have a brand *new* reality—that in Messiah, *"[we] are unleavened."*

બે ❦

Abba, teach me what it means to be unleavened—to be without sin. Thank You for setting me free, that I may live my life no longer bound to the ways of the flesh. Help me, Father, to live in newness of life; show me how to behave according to who I now really am. Lord, I praise You and bless Your great Name—teach me Your ways of purity and truth, that I may thrive in the salvation that is my true, new reality in You…

> "מַצָּה, *Matzah is to be eaten [throughout]
> the seven days, and* חָמֵץ, *chametz (anything
> leavened) is not [to be] seen with you; yes,
> leaven is not [to be] seen with you in all your
> territory."* שְׁמוֹת *Sh'mot (Exodus) 13:7*

During the Week of Matzah, we are commanded to "feast" on unleavened bread—we are reminded that we are free, having been redeemed and delivered into new life. We are also commanded to *fast* from anything made with *chametz*—leaven—which reminds us of our old life in bondage and affliction. But the command contains more than simply abstention from leavened food—in fact, we are not even to be *seen* with it *"in all your territory"* during these seven days.

There is a spiritual truth here that should not be lost on us: even if we do not *intend* to consume it, when we allow leaven—sin—to linger in our presence, its very existence and immutable ability to swell into unguarded places will eventually overcome us, and we will again succumb to its power. Though we have been set free from sin, we remain susceptible and vulnerable to its effects. We must therefore walk *deliberately* in our freedom so that we do not revert to our former ways.

So how can the Week of Matzah help us overcome the effects of sin?

For seven full days, we are feasting on matzah—reveling in our redemption and freedom, being reminded of our purely unleavened identity in Messiah. At the same time, we are abstaining from leaven—we have removed it completely from our lives, reminding us that we are able *and expected* to take an active role in keeping ourselves separated and sanctified from sin.

But this is not some *intellectual* reminder, written on a piece of paper and experienced only in our minds. It is a *vivid, tangible* reminder that we experience with all of our senses. Every part of our being is reminded of our new nature in Messiah.

By participating fully in the Feast of Matzah, we are given a divine opportunity to be graphically taught the reality of our freedom in Messiah—to learn how to live according to the new life we have in Him. The week of Matzah not only teaches us how to embrace purity and to abstain from sin, but also how to get away *and stay away* from the things that formerly held us captive. Since we are no longer bound by sin and the flesh, we need to realize that we don't have to return to our former ways—*ever*. So let us partake of the matzah, and let us be rid of the leaven—for we are truly *free...*

∂⌀ ⋘

Yeshua, You have set me free! Help me to continue to mature in You and grow further away from the person I used to be. Father, teach me to see myself in the matzah, that I will be reminded and encouraged that I am, in reality, unleavened. Abba, show me that I now have the ability to say "no" to sin and the flesh, and "yes" to who You have made me to be. I bless You and worship You, ADONAI, the one and only Matzah Maker...

Slaves to Righteousness

*"… and having been freed from sin,
you became slaves to righteousness."*
Romans 6:18

Sin had us in a stranglehold. We were bound to sin, slaves to its commands, unable to live a life for God. We couldn't see that sin owned us, yet we obeyed it, heeded its instruction, and submitted to its authority. We were helpless—we had no choice but to be enticed and entangled in sin…

But *"having been freed from sin, [we] became slaves to righteousness."*

Whether we know it or not, this is our reality in Messiah. Sin is no longer our owner because our new Master is Righteousness—we obey *Him*, heed *His* instruction, and submit to His authority alone. Yet we are kept from seeing or believing this reality because of the war that continues to wage in our flesh. We doubt our standing before God because we have watched ourselves dip again and again into the pool of our past selves. We are reminded of the sins in which we used to wallow… the flesh that once defined us.

As disciples of Messiah, we need to accept—once and for all—this new reality: no matter how our flesh behaves, we have been *"freed from sin,"* and become *"slaves to righteousness."* You may be in the process of falling away—you may have already fallen—but if you have truly been made alive to God in the Messiah Yeshua, you are no longer who you used to be... *you can change.*

Though our flesh may remain enslaved to sin, our new nature is free—a slave only to righteousness! Now, in Messiah, we may choose to no longer live in sin because the Righteous One has delivered us. We have been released from prison... we have been set free. Demand that your flesh fall in line with who you *really* are in Messiah, and partake of the old "leaven" no longer.

Yes, there *is* a war between the old "you" and the new. The question you need to ask yourself is, "Which side are you on?"

৶ ৶

Abba, Father, I struggle between my old self and who I truly am in You—I even know when I am sinning, but I can't seem to stop. ADONAI, I believe You have given me the ability to walk in newness of life right now—I know You have set me free from sin so that I can be a slave to righteousness. Teach me to walk in Your ways, O God; show me how to yield completely and only to You. I bless Your Name, ADONAI, for I can now choose to walk according to who I really am... and in You, I am brand new...

*"… [we] bring into captivity every
thought to [make it] obey the Messiah."*
2Corinthians 10:5b

As we patrol each day through this escalating
conflict called life, we are vulnerable—susceptible to the
temptations all around us. Though we have the mind of
Messiah and have been made new in Him, our flesh
remains in constant jeopardy from the unceasing
barrage against us. Every day, we are overtly and subtly
bombarded by thoughts and images from the world.
They do their best to infest our minds and violate our
inner being, enticing us to behave in ways contrary to
who we are in Messiah.

We are especially reminded of this during the Week
of Matzah. Even after we have both physically and
spiritually cleaned out the *chametz* (leaven),
unbeknownst to us, the crumbs of temptation still lurk
in secret crevasses we were unable to reach. Beckoning
to us in the hopes of luring us into sin once more, their
echoes resonate in our minds. They seem real… and
slowly, like a phantom, they begin to draw us back to
the thoughts of our old ways.

Against such attacks, our only hope is to bring *"into
captivity every thought to [make it] obey the Messiah."*
We cannot allow our thoughts to re-enslave us, but
instead we must turn the tables and take control of our
minds. We have to remember that sin and participation

in the flesh begin with entertaining—and then embracing—the thoughts that lead to sin. When we take every thought captive, not allowing ourselves to dwell on the memories of our former ways, we will not yield again to the yearnings of our flesh.

But not only must we take each thought captive, we must also *[make it] obey the Messiah.*" This is a spiritual act of warfare. We capture our thoughts by enslaving our minds to the Spirit. Then, as we remember who we truly are in Messiah and focus on His righteous ways, we are able to force each sinful notion into submission.

When the thoughts of the world begin to infiltrate our ranks, what will be our response? Will we befriend them and set them free, so that they can rally to terrorize us another day? Or will we take every single thought captive, and by the Spirit, "*[make it] obey*"?

৵৹ ৹৵

Abba, Father, teach me how to effectively take every thought captive and make it obey the Messiah. Give me the self-control and self-awareness to know what is happening in my mind and be able to submit it fully to You. I praise You, ADONAI, for You alone are the captor of men's minds and the deliverer of men's souls. Reveal to me my hidden temptations, Lord, that I may draw them out into the open and deal with them once and for all. Thank You, Abba, for maturing me and leading me to walk victoriously in Your freedom…

There Is Freedom

> *"… but whenever [the sons of Yis'rael] turn to ADONAI, the veil is taken away. Now ADONAI is the Spirit; and where the Spirit of ADONAI is, there is freedom. And we all, with unveiled face, beholding the glory of ADONAI [as] in a mirror, are being transformed into the same image, from glory to glory, even as by the Spirit of ADONAI." 2Corinthians 3:16-18*

When we as disciples of Messiah have difficulty seeing the things of God, we cannot blame the veil. The Master has taken away the veil that once covered our faces—He drew us and we turned to Him. From that moment on, the veil was lifted forever, and we have been able to see clearly. But having the *ability* to see does not necessarily mean that we actually *do* it. Indeed, even though the veil was taken away, perhaps we never realized that we are allowed to open our eyes!

"Where the Spirit of ADONAI is, there is freedom." Now that we are in Messiah, we have complete and total freedom. This is not the freedom to simply do whatever we please—it is freedom from sin and death. In Messiah, we are free to abide in the ways of life, holiness, godliness, purity and truth. Sin and death no longer bind us, and we are free to be alive in Him.

We are now in the process of *"being transformed into the same image"*—the image of the glory of ADONAI that we behold. As in a mirror, the glory of ADONAI is seen like a reflection; but with open eyes and unveiled faces, we now see that the reflection is our own! The veil has been taken away so that we can behold the glory of ADONAI and yield ourselves to the Spirit, for in Him alone there is freedom.

The Spirit of ADONAI takes us *"from glory to glory"*— ever increasing in our reflection of the glory of ADONAI. Year after year, the week of Matzah reminds us of this process. Each year, we have the opportunity to mark our lives and recommit ourselves to allowing ADONAI to bring us from one degree of maturity, prosperity, health, and understanding to the next. As we recognize and embrace the significance of this week and its purpose for our growth in the Lord, by the Spirit we will go from glory to glory, and we will rise to new heights of freedom in Messiah...

For ADONAI, the Spirit, has taken away the veil...

₧ ₨

ADONAI, Spirit, You have taken away the veil—now open my eyes, that I may see the freedom You have given to me. Teach me, Lord, to submit to Your ways, that I may allow You to mold me and recreate me according to Your will. I praise Your name, O God, for You have set me free that I may serve You. I bless Your name, Father, for You are my Savior; and as You transform me, I will go from glory to glory to glory...

Be Following Me

"*…and [during] the days of Unleavened Bread, [Herod] put [Keifa] in prison…. the same night,* כֵּיפָא*, Keifa was sleeping between two soldiers, having been bound with two chains— guards were also in front of the door watching the prison. And behold, a messenger of* ADONAI *[was suddenly] standing there, and a light shined in the buildings. And having struck* כֵּיפָא*, Keifa in the side, he woke him up, saying, 'Rise in haste,' and his chains fell from off his hands. The messenger also said to him, 'Gird yourself, and bind on your sandals;' and he did so, and [the messenger] said to him, 'Put your garment around [you] and be following me;' and having gone forth, [Keifa] followed him, and… having passed by the first and second guard, they came to the iron gate that leads into the city, which opened for them of its own accord…. And* כֵּיפָא*, Keifa having come to himself, said, 'Now I know of the truth: that* ADONAI *sent forth His messenger, and did deliver me…'" Acts 12:3b-11*

Realizing that he could earn political clout for the persecution of Messianic Jews, Herod imprisoned Keifa on a whim. Obviously not wanting to leave anything to chance, he put Keifa under heavy guard until he could be brought out for sentencing. Not only was the door of the prison being watched, but Keifa's hands were each bound with chains as he slept with a soldier on either side. There was no way that Keifa could avoid being another bloody cog in Herod's political wheel.

But even though this was a prison from which no man could escape, Herod didn't realize—and even Keifa didn't expect—that there was One who would have no trouble getting *in*. In a sudden burst of light, a messenger of ADONAI stood before Keifa... and in moments, his hands were free from his chains.

Keifa laid there blurry-eyed, the soldiers still on either side. No longer bound, his reality had changed—though his situation was not much improved. The bonds that had once held Keifa captive had been loosed, yet as long as he laid there, he was nothing more than a free man trapped inside a prison of his own making. Keifa was nearly free, but the only thing holding him back *now*... was himself.

In Messiah, our reality has changed. We are no longer bound by the chains of sin and death—we have been set free. But even though ADONAI can make the chains fall from our hands—even though He can make us invisible to our captors and cause gates to open before us of their own accord—if we do not *"rise in haste... gird [ourselves]... bind on [our] sandals... put our garment[s] around [us],"* and *follow Him,* we can never be truly free. Let us praise ADONAI that all our chains are broken. Then, let's once and for all walk out of our prisons the only possible way we can... *"rise in haste... and be following [Him]..."*

એ ૭

ADONAI, I magnify Your great Name! *"Now I know of the truth,"* that You have sent forth Your Son, *"and did deliver me."* I bless You, O Holy One, for You entered the prison from which no man could escape, that I might be set free. Thank You, ADONAI, for leading me into my deliverance. Hasten me, Lord, that I will not hesitate to follow in the way of Your Salvation....

> *"In the freedom, then, with which Messiah has made you free—stand!—and be not held fast again by a yoke of slavery." Galatians 5:1*

As we conclude the Week of Matzah—the commemoration of Yis'rael's exodus from *Mitz'rayim* (Egypt)—perhaps it is a good time to recall the words ADONAI spoke to us so long ago. As we cowered in fear between the Sea and the pursuing army, ADONAI spoke to us through His servant, *"Fear not! Still yourselves, and see the salvation of ADONAI, which He does for you today. For as you have seen the מִצְרַיִם, Mitz'rayim today, you will never see them again…" (Sh'mot 14:13)*

As disciples of Messiah, our identity is also reflected in this defining moment for Yis'rael. *Mitz'rayim* is our past—the sin to which we were once enslaved and oppressed; the Sea before us, our future—a pathway of faith leading to salvation. Will we trust that He will make a way where there seems to be no way? Will we step into the Sea to see our Savior? Today we have a choice before us much like that of our forefathers: will we heed the voice of ADONAI and stand still in His salvation, or will we lose our nerve and return to *Mitz'rayim*, being *"held fast again by a yoke of slavery?"*

This week, we have had a unique opportunity to be reminded of our freedom in Messiah. We have spent these last seven days feasting on our redemption (*matzah*), while fasting from our sins (*chametz*). Let us now allow the Spirit to seal this discipline in our hearts and minds, that we may celebrate and remember the freedom we have in Messiah every single day.

"In the freedom, then, with which Messiah has made you free—stand!"—pure, holy, and unleavened. You were not brought to the edge of the Sea, only to drown or be dragged away in chains. Don't let yourself be tied up again with a yoke of slavery to sin and the flesh. Instead, stand! Enslave yourself to the Master, walk confidently through the Sea with faith, and allow Him to remake you on the other side once again. *"Still yourselves, and see the salvation of ADONAI, which He does for you today."* He has delivered you—and those Egyptians are ancient history...

ॐ ๙

Abba, Father, thank You for this week of being dedicated and sanctified to You. I bless Your Name, ADONAI, for You have shown me once again what it means to be truly free. I praise You, Lord, for teaching me to be mindful of You during this next season—to be vigilant and diligent as I daily watch Your steady hand at work in my life. Teach me, O God, to stand firm in Your faithful salvation, that I may mature and thrive within the borders of Your abounding, endless freedom....

For Your Acceptance

"Speak to the sons of יִשְׂרָאֵל, Yis'rael, and you will say to them, 'When you come into the land which I am giving to you, and have reaped its harvest, and brought in the עֹמֶר, omer (sheaf)—the beginning of your harvest to the כֹּהֵן, cohen—then he will wave the עֹמֶר, omer before ADONAI for your acceptance...'" וַיִּקְרָא Vayik'ra (Leviticus) 23:10-11

The sons of Yis'rael were freed from slavery in *Mitz'rayim.* ADONAI brought them out of bondage to fulfill His promise—to deliver the sons of Yis'rael into the Land of their Fathers. There, Yis'rael would find an abundant country that would yield its plentiful crops in season.

After forty years in the desert, eating nothing but manna, surely the sons of Yis'rael were anxious to taste the fruit of that first harvest. But ADONAI gave one requirement regarding the harvest: both that first year, and every Spring thereafter, Yis'rael was to bring an *omer* from the harvest to the *cohen.* Accompanied by grain and burnt offerings, the *omer* was to be presented to ADONAI—a sacrifice of thanks for a rich season of bountiful harvest.

But this was not to be just any *omer*—it was to be from *"the beginning of your harvest."* Before even tasting the first harvest of the year, Yis'rael was to bring the first sheaf to Adonai. It could not be held back or used for some other purpose, and no other *omer* could take its place. The first *omer* was the harvest's special representative, reserved for Adonai alone.

When the *omer* was brought to the *cohen*, he was to *"wave the omer before Adonai."* By lifting up the harvest's representative *omer* to the Lord, it became a symbolic offering for the *entire* harvest *"for your acceptance...."* In order for Yis'rael to be acceptable to Adonai, an offering for the harvest—a specially dedicated offering—had to be made.

During this season, as we count from the day the first *omer* was to be waved, let us also allow *ourselves* to be waved before Adonai as the first of a great harvest yet to come. Let us not hold ourselves back or devote ourselves to some other purpose, but be fully dedicated to Adonai, that an abundant crop may be harvested through *us*. As Yeshua's special representatives, may we be lifted up and waved before Adonai for all the peoples—first, the Jew, and then the nations—for the reaping of a harvest, and for our acceptance....

৵ ৵

Adonai, I present myself to You, that my life may be lifted up and waved before You as an acceptable offering. Father, grow me and mature me, that I may truly be Your special representative—an effective disciple of my Master. I bless Your Name, Adonai, for You alone can deem me "acceptable," and receive me as the first of a harvest yet to come. Teach me Your ways, Adonai, that I may grow strong and tall in You—and in the days and weeks ahead, may You reap a bountiful harvest in me....

"But other [seed] fell to the good ground, and produced fruit, sprouting up and increasing, and it grew—one thirty-fold, and one sixty, and one a hundred [times what was sown]." Mark 4:8

One of the reasons we as disciples of Messiah do not grow and mature in our walk with Him is because we expect the impossible. We expect God to do a radical transformation of our lives and make all of our problems instantly go away. ADONAI does indeed change us, and He can do so in the blink of an eye—yet He does not do this according to our design, but to His.

If we had our way, we would enter into a relationship with the Lord holding on to all of our previous experiences. We would emerge on the other side of a dramatic transformation with all those experiences still intact—the only difference being that we would somehow be holier or less sinful from that point forward. In reality, however, God does not change us and then have us pick up our lives from the moment we left off. We are supposed to die, and then be born again—we have to start over.

All of us want to be the seed that falls into rich soil and produces grain—but we want it now, no waiting. We want to go from little seeds that have had no nurturing or sustenance, to suddenly and miraculously becoming mature and fully functioning believers. But in God's economy, the seed needs to sit in the ground for a while, growing and maturing as it hides beneath the surface. Then, one day, it emerges—not as a mature stalk, but as a tiny, fragile sprout. Over an extended period of time, that sprout grows; and only when it reaches full maturity does it yield a harvest.

It is not by coincidence or convenience that our maturing process can be likened to a crop on its agricultural schedule. Like the crops, we cannot rush things along by artificial means—we must yield ourselves completely and allow ADONAI to mature us in *His* timing. When we grow to maturity, we will bring forth our fruit and yield a crop beyond our expectations—*"thirty-fold... sixty... a hundred [times what was sown]..."*

ॐ ॐ

ADONAI, I yield myself fully to You. Remove from my heart any agendas or ideas that *I* can move *You* along in my maturing process. I joyfully resign myself to Your masterful ways, and I await the nurturing of Your Gardener's hand. I praise You, Father, for planting deep inside me the desire to live for You. I bless Your Name, for You have plans to grow in me thirty, sixty, even a hundred times what I could have ever sown alone....

"And it will be, because you hear these judgments, and will keep and do them, that ADONAI your God will keep to you the covenant and the kindness which He has sworn to your fathers. [He] will love you, and bless you, and multiply you, and will bless the fruit of your womb, and the fruit of your ground, your grain, and your new wine, and your oil, the increase of your oxen, and the wealth of your flock, in the land which He has sworn to your fathers to give to you." דְּבָרִים *D'variym (Deuteronomy) 7:12-13*

The stipulations for the covenant that ADONAI cut with Yis'rael are simple: listen to, keep and obey the judgments of ADONAI, and He will love you—that is, He will bless you and give you increase. As we grow and mature in our faith by hearing His words, keeping them and doing them, surely we can expect ADONAI's blessings to be poured out upon us. We need to realize, however, that those blessing may not be exactly what we expect.

When ADONAI blesses us, it is not with adornments or other non-utilitarian embellishments. Being blessed does not mean that we have discretionary income, extravagant things, and everything we ever thought we wanted. For ADONAI, blessing His people means giving them the essentials of life—and giving *those* things in great abundance. If we are truly to appreciate ADONAI's blessings, we would do well to shed the shackles of worldly trappings and other things that we had once mistakenly labeled as "important."

ADONAI's promises are simple—He will bless the fruit of our bodies, the fruit of our ground, and the fruit of our labor. Make no mistake, there is great truth here. We cannot look at our ancestors of old and think that God chose to bless them with such simple things merely because they were simple people with simple needs. On the contrary, ADONAI's design for His holy ones in *all* generations was that *we* would be simple people with simple needs. Complexity of life is not from Him—it is a byproduct of our "civilized" living.

When we allow ourselves to get caught up in the self-made intricacies of life, our values and priorities become confused. Living according to the Scriptures enables us to be objective—to not embrace the values and priorities of the world, but of the Lord. We may live in a "civilized" society, but that does not negate the truth that ADONAI has called us to live as simple people who are not caught up in the ways of the world. As we count these days from the *omer*, let us allow the Lord to distance us from the unimportant things of life. It's time to get back to the basics, where being blessed simply means that we have plenty of only what we need....

ADONAI, purify me—separate me from the trappings of my life. Lord, show me the areas of my life that are truly unimportant—help me to push them aside, and replace them with the essentials of living a holy life for You. I bless You, Abba, Father, for loving me and giving me increase according to Your definition alone. I praise Your Name, ADONAI, my perfect provider....

1% You

"*And* ADONAI *said to* גִּדְעוֹן, *Gid'on, 'Too
many* are *the people who* are *with you for My
giving* מִדְיָן, *Mid'yan into their hand, lest*
יִשְׂרָאֵל, *Yis'rael glorify itself against Me, saying,
"[By] my [own] hand has salvation been given to
me..."' And* ADONAI *said to [Gid'on], 'Everyone
who laps the water with his tongue as a dog laps,
you are to set him apart...' And the number of
those lapping... was three hundred.... And*
ADONAI *said to* גִּדְעוֹן, *Gid'on, 'By the three
hundred men who are lapping, I [will] save you
and will give* מִדְיָן, *Mid'yan into your hand.'*"
שֹׁפְטִים *Shof'tiym (Judges) 7:2, 5-7*

Too often, we give in to our doubts and fears,
believing that ADONAI cannot or will not continue to save
us. These fears are not only rooted in our lack of faith in
Him, but they also spring from our own arrogance. True
faith requires zero self-reliance. We need to understand
that total deliverance is birthed from complete
dependence on ADONAI. Indeed, our participation in
our own salvation is minimal—all we have to do is
accept and submit.

When Gid'on set out to fight Mid'yan, he had over
30,000 men... but then ADONAI began to send them
home. Of the ten thousand who were unafraid to face
Mid'yan, ADONAI chose a mere 300 to complete the
task—just 1% of the original fighting force. Why did
God do this? So that Yis'rael would not be able to boast
against ADONAI saying, "*[By] my [own] hand has*

salvation been given to me." ADONAI's process of elimination speaks to His sovereign ability to save: not only did He *not* need thousands, but the few hundred that remained were chosen because of their remarkable, dog-like qualities.

Our natural inclination is to enter a difficult situation decked out for war. We don our strongest armor and take tens of thousands of our best warriors with us. We bring tons of artillery and great weapons of destruction to pulverize the enemy with sheer might. We strategize and make provision for all contingencies, and we psych ourselves up for the battle. Now imagine standing before an enemy horde, naked and alone, holding only a box of rubber bands and some paper clips. This was Gid'on.

We will not win the battles before us because we possess the strength to do it. On the contrary, victory in Messiah is at best 1% us—but in reality, *it's all Him.* The Lord will use us as we are, dog-like and all. He will work in our lives in ways that we don't expect or even think are possible. What we bring to the table in our relationship with God is of no consequence where our salvation is concerned. He does not ask us to take control of or manage our deliverance—He wants us to let Him complete us, save us… and then deliver our enemies into our hands.

❧ ❧

ADONAI, forgive my arrogance. Teach me, God, to rely solely on You—to put no stock in my ability to provide for or protect myself. Abba, only You can build a winning army of three hundred from thirty thousand. Show me how to present myself before You, the dog that I am, and know that I am clean and worthy of being used by Your mighty hand. I bless Your Name, ADONAI, for only by *Your* strength am I saved….

You Have Probed

> *"You have probed my heart, You have visited [me] by night, You have tested me, finding nothing [against me]. My [sinful] thoughts pass not over my lips."*
> תְּהִלִּם *T'hillim (Psalms) 17:3*

A good doctor takes an active interest in his patients. After he performs a procedure, he will conduct follow-up visits to monitor the patient's progress. As disciples of Messiah, we too have regular examinations, as the Lord observes our general state of health and the development of our maturity and refinement.

Since undergoing The Surgery, the Lord continues to schedule and perform various tests on us. Our responsibility is simply to submit and respond to His instructions so that we don't hinder any ongoing rehabilitation. He begins each session by probing our heart to check its condition. Are we holding fast to the new life implanted in us, or are we beginning to show signs of rejection? Does our heart have integrity—are there any holes or damage that need repair?

After the exam, He sends us home… but then He visits us at night—and it is a revealing test. During the day, when we are awake and aware, we modify our behavior in an attempt to camouflage any outward signs of trouble. But as we sleep—when we can no longer exert control over what we think and how we feel—

everything is revealed. The Surgeon is not so concerned with how we are doing outwardly as with what is happening on the inside, for He knows that a submissive mind and a humble heart will produce obedient behavior. He continues to probe.

ADONAI tests us, searching our hearts, looking for potential health risks or signs of disease. Our hope, when the examination is complete, is that He finds nothing wrong—we receive a clean bill of health. Should He ever find *"[sinful] thoughts [passing] over [our] lips,"* it will be a telltale sign that additional coronary procedures may be necessary. But as long as He finds nothing against us, we can be sure that our regimen of purification and holiness is taking hold, and we are growing strong.

Since The Surgery, a change in us has already begun. It started the moment Yeshua was revealed to us, and it continues day after day as we strengthen our heart though the regular exercise of our freedom in Messiah. There will be times when we will have to go back under the knife in order to clean things up and make them function as they should, for it takes time to completely replace such a delicate, soft machine as the heart. And when the time comes, we must do our part—to hold still, so that the steady hand of The Surgeon may do His masterful work....

૭ ૭

ADONAI, may I pass Your exams with flying colors! Teach me, Lord, to continually submit to Your ways. May my heart and mind possess the integrity needed to fully contain the new life You have given me. Continue to work in me, Abba, Father, that I will be able to accept corrections and adjustments according to Your prescription. I bless Your Name for Your skillfulness to change me... and to make me new all over again.

Grow Up

*"… we will in all [ways] grow up into
Him, who is the head—the Messiah."*
Ephesians 4:15

When my oldest son was three years old, someone asked him what he wanted to be when he grew up. To spark his imagination, he was given an extensive list of possible vocations, ranging from doctor to cowboy. This sent my son the message that the world is his oyster, and he can do and be whatever he wants—just as soon as he grows up. But does our freedom in Messiah give us the right to do and be *whatever we want*?

The Scriptures are not so haphazard in giving us direction for our lives. They certainly do not present us with the vague formula many of us as middle-class Americans teach our kids as they get older: go to school, get good grades, and stay out of trouble… go to college, get good grades, and stay out of trouble… get a good job, make some money, and—when you think you can afford it—get married… make some more money so you can get a mortgage, and—when you think you can afford it—have some kids… keep making money, be a good person, and stay out of trouble.

On the contrary, the Scriptures give us a very clear directive: "in *all [ways] grow up into Him, who is the head—the Messiah."* Our faith and trust in Yeshua forms the basis for our value system—both the foundation and the goal is Messiah, and everything we do has Him as our aim. Yes, in Messiah we have freedom, but not the kind of freedom that lets us do whatever we want. Living according to what we want and desire is not freedom—it's *independence*, and the Scriptures never teach us to be independent. Just the opposite, the Scriptures direct us to unite together under the headship of Messiah, *dependant* both on the Master and on one other.

Messiah alone is our standard. He models and exemplifies holiness and godliness as embodied in the Scriptures, and this gives us a practical plumb line from which to discern our own level of growth and maturity. We are to grow up into Him; that is, to mature into the fullness of the new creation we have already been made to be. We are "in Messiah" by virtue of our regeneration. Now we are called to practically live out that reality.

What do you want to be when you grow up? I want to be like Messiah….

                       ᔦ ᕬ

Master, in every area of my life, make me like You. Teach me the ways of Your Word, that I may submit my life and conform to Your likeness. Lord, show me the freedom of abounding in You, the liberty of being set apart and holy for You. I bless Your Name, for You are my Master, the head of my life. Thank You, Lord, for causing me to grow up into You….

To Be Blameless In Holiness

"And you, [may] the Lord cause
[you] to increase and to overflow in love
toward one another and toward everyone,
even as we also [do] toward you; toward
the strengthening [of] your hearts [to be]
blameless in holiness before our God and
Father at the coming of our Master
Yeshua with all His holy ones."
1Thessalonians 3:12-13

ADONAI's desire for us is that one day, at the coming
of our Master Yeshua, we will stand *"blameless in
holiness before our God and Father."* But by what means
does He expect us to arrive in such a pristine state?
Given our present, lowly circumstances, how can we
hope to achieve such a lofty and immaculate condition?
Surely, the Lord plans on doing something rather
drastic with us in order to make us worthy to appear
before Him *"with all His holy ones."*

When we think of holiness, we usually equate it with
degrees of *sinlessness.* In other words, we think we are
holy when we refuse to act on our desires—and we
think that to be *really* holy we need to achieve the
ethereal state of no longer even *having* desires at all. But
Paul shows us that holiness can be much more *human*
than that. Paul indicates that holiness is present when

"the Lord [causes us] to increase and to overflow in love toward one another and toward everyone."

Only when we increase and overflow in such love will we receive *"the strengthening [of our] hearts [to be] blameless."* When our hearts are weak, we are too easily led away into sin. Strengthening in blamelessness comes as we take the focus off ourselves and pour out love toward one another. We are holy, not simply because we keep ourselves from sinning, but because we give away the love in our hearts—we walk the way the Master walks; we love the way the Master loves.

Being holy is not just a matter of being on our best behavior—it requires our submission and active surrender to the Holy One. We do not automatically possess the inner strength to be blameless because of anything we do or think—it is the Lord alone who makes holiness grow and abound in our lives. Let us choose to submit to and walk in God's ways, and then yield ourselves fully to Him who *"causes [us] to increase and to overflow in love… toward the strengthening [of our] hearts [to be] blameless in holiness."*

২৯ ৺৯

Abba, I yield myself completely to You. I bless Your Holy Name, for You make me increase and overflow in love, that my heart may be strengthened. Show me Your ways, O Holy One, for I desire only to walk in blamelessness. You are worthy to receive all praise, for You alone can cause me to abound in love. Father, I welcome Your refining hand. Make me holy Lord, as You alone are holy…

Go On to Maturity

> *"Therefore, having left [behind] the elementary teaching about the Messiah, let us go on to maturity, not again laying a foundation of reformation from dead works, and of faith in God, of the teaching about washings, also of laying on of hands, also of rising again from the dead, and of eternal judgment."* עִבְרִים *Iv'riym (Hebrews) 6:1-2*

Our faith is founded on *"the elementary teaching about Messiah"*—the simple, basic truths about the Master. The Letter Writer, however, exhorts us to leave these teachings behind once we have learned them, and to *"go on to maturity, not again laying a foundation…"* These *"elementary teachings"* form the basis for our faith, giving us a seedbed in which to take root and grow. So why is it so difficult for us to *"go on to maturity?"* Why is it so hard to develop and mature in Messiah?

Perhaps part of the difficulty is that we continue to lay our foundations over and over again. Rather than learning things the first time so that we can move on, we forget what we have learned and have to keep going back over the rudimentary things of Messiah. It is one thing to be diligent in keeping the simple truths of God before us, but it is another thing altogether to keep relearning what should have become completely apparent and natural to us by now.

On the other hand, sometimes we are perfectly willing to leave behind *"the elementary teaching about the Messiah"*—but instead of going on to maturity, we *ignore* the foundational things and believe we are too mature to revisit them. Out of this comes the invention of our own personal set of beliefs and religions— strange doctrines that do not hold up to the litmus test of Scripture. Without being tethered to the fundamental truths of the faith, we run amuck—we think that we are mature when we are only misguided.

With regard to maturing in the Lord, we must remember this simple truth: maturity comes from building on the foundation, which is Messiah. If we fail to build on Messiah, or if we build on anything other than Him, we will not go on to maturity. There is one foundation and one goal, and it is the One and Only— Yeshua, our Messiah. If the foundation fails to be established, we have no hope. Let us therefore build on the *"elementary teaching about the Messiah,"* so that we can go on to maturity and grow up into Him.

కు ఇ

Lord, help me to once and for all learn the *"elementary teachings"* about You. Show me how to make those lessons a part of me, that I may graduate to the next level. Abba, teach me how to not keep laying again the foundation, but to go on to maturity and be a full-grown, healthy, functioning vessel for Your kingdom. I bless You, ADONAI, for You lead me into the simple things of Your Word. Thank You, ADONAI, my Teacher....

> *"…and [for] this same [reason] also—*
> *besides having brought in all diligence—*
> *superadd to your faith, virtue; and to virtue,*
> *knowledge; and to knowledge, self-control; and*
> *to self-control, perseverance; and to*
> *perseverance, godliness; and to godliness,*
> *brotherly affection; and to brotherly affection,*
> *love. For [if] you have these things abound to*
> *you,* you *will be neither lazy nor unfruitful in*
> *regard to the acknowledging of our Master*
> *Yeshua [the] Messiah."* כֵּיפָא ב *Keifa Beit*
> *(2Peter) 1:5-8*

As we walk day by day according to the Spirit, we are enjoined to bear spiritual fruit—love, joy, peace, patience, kindness, goodness, faithfulness, humility, and self-control (Galatians 5). These are the fruits produced in us as we submit fully to ADONAI and His Word by the Spirit. But bearing such fruit is not simply a matter of planting a seed and watching it grow. On the contrary, we reap an abundant harvest by first cultivating the qualities that *lead us* into fruitfulness. It is these characteristics that Keifa admonishes us to *"superadd"* to our faith—one quality upon another—that we may grow into vital, fruitful disciples of Messiah.

Consider the farmer who takes great care in ensuring the health and growth of his crops. Does he pray they will receive rain, while sheltering them from the sunlight? Does he allow plenty of sun, but starve them of nutrients from the soil? Does he provide them with supplements and food, yet leave them parched and dying of thirst? Such would be foolishness, yielding nothing but death— an empty, worthless crop. The same may be said of us when we do not *"superadd"* to our faith the qualities that lead us into fruitfulness.

Just as a crop needs not just one, but *all* the right conditions to grow and reach its fullest potential, so do we as disciples of Messiah need to be properly nourished in our faith. It is insufficient to have faith without virtue; knowledge without self-control; perseverance without godliness; brotherly affection without love. Instead, we are exhorted to add to and supply our faith with these ever-increasing qualities—food for the hungry, drink for the thirsty, light in the darkness.

ADONAI has given us everything we need to avoid being *"lazy [and] unfruitful in regard to the acknowledging of our Master Yeshua [the] Messiah."* Not only do we have the right seed, but we have been blessed with the ideal conditions to plant an orchard of great faithfulness. Will we now till the ground and work the fields, so that we may abundantly bear the qualities and characteristics of a mature disciple of Messiah? The choice is ours—to leave the land to fend for itself; or to pick up our tools, nurture the crops, and get to work….

వ ఈ

Abba, Father, I bless Your Name—help me to superadd to my faith the qualities that will lead me into maturity. Teach me to submit to Your masterful ways, ADONAI, that I may be abundantly fruitful for You. I praise Your name, O God, for You do not leave me barren. Sow your gracious work in me, that I may grow and abound in You. I yield myself to You, Mighty God, keeper and nourisher of my soul…

*"And the sin of the young men was
very great in ADONAI's presence… but
שְׁמוּאֵל, Sh'muel was ministering in the
presence of ADONAI… and the young [boy]
שְׁמוּאֵל, Sh'muel grew up with ADONAI….
[and] kept going on and growing in good
[favor] both with ADONAI, and also with
men…. And שְׁמוּאֵל, Sh'muel grew up, and
ADONAI had been with him [all along],
and did not let fall any of his words to the
[ground of the] earth."* א שְׁמוּאֵל *Sh'muel
Alef (1 Samuel) 2:17-18, 21, 26; 3:19*

When we were young, we thought we knew
everything—and some of us think we still do. We were
convinced that we could get away with pretty much
anything we wanted. If we glanced around and didn't see
anyone, we were sure that we were "safe"—that no one
could see what we were about to do. Hopefully, we've
come to learn just how wrong we were—that we're
always being watched… that Someone can *always* see.

The other young *co'haniym* were sinning greatly "in
ADONAI's *presence*." As they ministered to their own
fleshly desires, they must have thought that ADONAI was
blind. But even from his youth, Sh'muel understood that
"in *the presence of* ADONAI," we have a choice: we can
minister to ourselves or to Him. Sh'muel took seriously
the task and privilege of ministering to the Lord—and as
he remained dedicated to and focused on ADONAI's
service, Sh'muel was kept from sin.

Messianic Mo'adiym Devotional **35**

The choices we make as we abide in ADONAI's presence will have consequences. If we choose to bask in His presence like the sons of Eli—taking Him for granted, exploiting His blessings, and using Him only to please ourselves—our time of strength will be cut short. But if we choose to minister in His presence—growing up with Him, and allowing His presence to prepare us for the ultimate service of His choosing—then we will find favor both with God and men. As we submit ourselves to His service, He will *"[be] with [us all along]"* the way. He will not abandon or allow us to fall, but will lead us into maturity.

Whether we are children becoming adults, or new disciples becoming seasoned ones, the choice remains before us: are we just going to keep growing *older*... or are we going to start growing *up*? ADONAI wants us to *"[keep] going on and growing in good [favor] both with [Him], and also with men."* Today, let us decide to no longer just *take* from His presence, but to give back from what we receive—that we may be kept safe from sin, and finally go on and grow up in Him...

Father, I praise You, for You are with me all along. Forgive me, Abba, for sinning in Your presence—for failing to see Your holiness before me. ADONAI, I bless Your Name; do not allow me to grow old without ever growing up. Teach me Your ways, O Lord, that none of my words may fall to the ground. May I go on—moving always closer to You... and grow up—moving further away from me....

"*…You—what you sow is not made
alive unless it dies; and that which you
sow, you sow not the body that will be, but
bare grain….*" 1Corinthians 15:36-37

In the end, our corruptible bodies will be sown in
death—yet they will be raised to life incorruptible.
They will be sown in dishonor, yet raised in glory; sown
a natural body, yet raised a spiritual one. But until that
Day, we are faced with the task of dying daily. Only
then will our lives in Messiah come alive *today*, that we
may reap the harvest of new life tomorrow.

Too often, we as believers in Messiah are reluctant
to give up our lives for Him. We yearn to walk in the
ways of our Master—the ways of salvation, power, and
peace—yet we are unwilling to sacrifice *our* lives for the
sake of living *His*. We invite the things of the past to
accompany us as we attempt to construct our new life
within the framework of the old. As a result, we confine
Yeshua to the comfortable corner we have set aside for
Him, and consult with Him only when it is convenient
and suits our needs.

As long as the Master remains compartmentalized
in the life we have made for ourselves, we will never be
"*made alive*" in Him. No matter how much we sow in
hope and prayer, asking God to deliver us from our
troubles, eradicate our enemies, and change our lives,
"*what [we] sow [will] not [be] made alive unless it dies.*"

Until we are willing to die daily to who we used to be—even to the parts of our old life that we would really like to keep around—a life of fruitfulness in Messiah will be forever beyond our reach.

To live in Messiah, we must sow ourselves in death. In that grave, we are to leave everything—good and bad—*"sow[ing] not the body that will be, but bare grain."* The *"body that will be"* grows from the seed sown in nakedness—no façades, no baggage, and no expectations... save the expectation that we *will* be made alive in Messiah.

What fruit will we bear—what harvest will we reap—as long as we remain alive to ourselves? Indeed, what kind of life can it be... *"unless it dies..."*?

৵ ৶

My Master, Yeshua, forgive me for putting You in my pocket—for thinking wrongly that *Your* job is to serve *my* life. Right now, O God, I release my own life and allow it to die, that I may be made alive only in You. I praise You, ADONAI, for You give back so much more than I could have ever brought with me. I bless You, my Master, for my *"body that will be"* when I am finally willing to die daily for You....

Pure Milk

"…as newborn babies, desire the Word's pure milk, [so] that by it you may grow into salvation." כֵּיפָא א *Keifa Alef* (1Peter) 2:2

Responsible parents take great care to protect and provide for their newborn child. They make sure that the baby's new environment is safe, comfortable, and— especially—clean. They are careful not to expose the infant to things that could introduce foreign bacteria or disease into the baby's precious little body. But one of the best ways to protect a baby *for life* is to give him the healthiest, strongest immune system possible. Until a baby is ready to eat solid food, a primary factor in building immunity is for the newborn to consume *only* his Mother's milk.

For a variety of reasons, many parents start their babies on "formula" from the very beginning. While the idea of giving a baby formula is not wrong in and of itself, there is no true replacement for pure milk that comes straight from Mama—everything else is just a substitute. No matter how close it may be to the original, or how much it succeeds in nourishing the child, nothing can perfectly replace the God-designed function of a mother feeding her baby from her own body.

This is *"the Word's pure milk"* that we are exhorted to desire. Keifa's point is not that we need to be bottle-fed the Word because we are immature, but that we should suckle on the Word as a newborn baby latches on to his mother's breast. It is life, it is satisfying, it is comforting, and it is pure. There is no opportunity for that pure milk to become tainted—it goes directly from the source into the thirsty mouth of the suckling child.

"The Word's pure milk" nourishes us naturally as God intended. By its purity, we build a strong resistance to infection, we are quicker to heal, and we are not easily brought down by the things around us. This is how we are able to *"grow into salvation"*—we thrive because we were given something pure from the moment we left the womb.

Without the untainted Word inside us, we cannot grow into the fullness of what God has for us. All too often, we become sick—our bodies are unable to withstand illness—because we did not get the strength and protection we needed from the beginning. The Good News is that Abba gives us the gift of *rebirth*, and *"as newborn babies,"* we can begin... again...

૭ৡ ৡ૭

Abba, teach me to look to You as a newborn baby looks to his mother. Make me unable to nourish myself with any kind of substitute, but let me be thirsty for and satisfied only by the pure milk of Your Word. May I be unable to digest anything else; cause me to cry out and not be comforted until You come to me. Teach me to rely on You alone for my life, ADONAI. I bless Your Name, Holy One, Giver and Sustainer of New Life....

All the Ways

"And you are to remember all the ways [in] which ADONAI your God has led you these forty years in the wilderness, in order to humble you and to test you, to know that which is in your heart— whether you will keep His commands or not." דְּבָרִים D'variym (Deuteronomy) 8:2

Because we don't always understand how ADONAI operates in our lives, we question whether or not He really knows what He's doing. But the truth is that He *always* knows what He's doing—and He works in our lives despite our inability to comprehend. This was definitely the case with the sons of Yis'rael as they roamed the desert before entering the Promised Land. As a generation, Yis'rael was wandering aimlessly and being systematically done away with—yet in reality, ADONAI was *leading* them the whole way.

In His sovereignty, ADONAI could have simply decided to bar Yis'rael from the Promised Land and ignore them until a whole generation was dead and gone. But instead, ADONAI "led [them those] forty years in the wilderness, in order to humble [them] and to test [them]." Though it may not have seemed so at the time, the humbling and testing that Yis'rael endured was for their deliberate discipleship as a people devoted to God. To Yis'rael, those years may have appeared pointless and helpless, filled with trouble and chastisement—and yet these were *"all the ways [in] which ADONAI [their] God [had] led [them]…"*

As disciples of Messiah, ADONAI also chooses to lead us through humbling and testing. His goal for these times is not our punishment and discipline—though without them we would surely persist in our old ways. Rather, He humbles us with a very specific purpose in mind: *"to know that which is in [our] heart[s]."* Through testing, ADONAI sees how our hearts are responding to Him—are we resisting His will, or learning our lessons? Like Yis'rael, our humbling leads us to a point of decision—*"whether [we] will keep His commands or not."*

Our ability to yield and submit to the ways of ADONAI is determined by how we allow the Lord to lead us *"in the wilderness."* When we make ourselves rigid out of obstinance or fear, times of testing will lead us into greater chastisement and discipline. But when we are pliable in the Maker's hands, the Lord's humbling ways will lead us only into maturity and times of fruitfulness. We do not need to—nor are we able to—fully comprehend the ways of our Creator. Yet we can always trust His loving hand of correction, relying on Him to straighten us out in the end….

ॐ ॐ

Abba, Father, I welcome Your humbling and testing. I submit to You, O God, for even when I do not understand what You are doing, I trust that You are leading me into fullness of life. Teach me to remember all the ways in which You lead me, Lord, so that I will never resist. I desire only Your firm, yet loving hand. Thank You, Father, for knowing what is in my heart. I bless Your Name, for You faithfully lead me… even when I am reluctant to go….

"*And the child [Yochanan (John) the Immerser] grew, and was strengthened in spirit, and he was in the wilderness until the day of his [public] appearance to Yis'rael.*" Luke 1:80

As we grow, both physically and spiritually, one of the main characteristics we need to nurture is *patience*. During times of development, all things must wait for the natural processes to run their course—or they risk stunting their own growth. A premature gathering of crops, for instance, will result in both an inadequate harvest and the endangerment of potential, future increase. As disciples of Messiah, we bear the fruit of patience by submitting ourselves to ADONAI's schedule, trusting that He is providing everything we need to ripen in due time.

Yochanan was not born immersing people in the Jordan River. Though destined to be the powerful forerunner of our Master, Yeshua, he first had to grow and be "*strengthened in spirit.*" Did Yochanan need this time of growth merely to gain specific knowledge or gather certain information? On the contrary, it was for the development of his *character*—to make him ready to enter into the fullness of his calling. In order to grow and be "*strengthened in spirit,*" Yochanan had to undergo a time of inner fortification—Yochanan had to *wait in the wilderness.*

Our "wilderness experiences" are for this very purpose—to strengthen our spirits. All too often, we allow our busy lives to distract us from being in ADONAI's presence. Because of this, He needs to get us alone so that He can have our full attention—and it is during these times that He builds our character, shaping us into vessels who may be entrusted with His message. When the day finally comes for us to emerge from the wilderness, we will find that we have indeed grown and been strengthened.

When we become strong in spirit, it is time for our "*[public] appearance.*" If we don't allow ourselves to get ahead of the Lord, we will never attempt to "appear" in public before we are ready. But when our days in the wilderness are over, we cannot wait—we must boldly speak the message of Yeshua.

ADONAI wants to make you famous! He has a plan for giving you an influential forum in which to proclaim the life-changing truth of the Kingdom of God—not just with your words, but with your life. Be patient, for you are being strengthened in spirit, and the time of your "*[public] appearance*" is at hand....

る め

Lord, make me grow and become strong in spirit. ADONAI, teach me the importance of submission and how to be patient—watching and waiting for You. I praise Your Name, O God, for You hold my whole life in Your hands. Show me, Lord, how to be at peace with this reality—to have faith that only You can direct my steps in the way I should go. When the time finally comes for my "*[public] appearance,*" help me to boldly speak Your truth. I bless Your great Name, Father, Giver of Strength, Teacher of Patience....

Two Sticks

"And [Eliyahu]… came to the city gate, and saw
there a widow woman gathering sticks. He called to
her and said, 'Bring to me, please, a little water in a
container that I [may] drink.' And she went and
brought it, and he called to her [again] and said,
'Bring to me, please, a morsel of bread in your hand.'
And she said, '[As] ADONAI your God lives, I have no
cake—only a handful of meal in a jar, and a little oil
in a dish. Look, I am gathering two sticks, that [I]
may go in and prepare it for myself and for my son—
we will eat it, then die.' And אֵלִיָּהוּ, Eliyahu said to
her, 'Fear not! Go [and] do according to your word,
but first, go make me a little cake, and have [it]
brought out to me—make [food] for you and for your
son last. For this [is what] ADONAI, God of
יִשְׂרָאֵל, Yis'rael says: 'The jar of meal will not be used
up, and the dish of oil will not [be] lacking until the
day ADONAI gives rain on the surface of the ground.'
So she went and did according to the word of
אֵלִיָּהוּ, Eliyahu, and she ate—she and he, and her
household—[for many] days." א מְלָכִים M'lachiym
Alef (1Kings) 17:10-15

When Eliyahu asked for a drink of water, the widow
obliged. But when He requested a morsel of bread, she
replied with a lament all too familiar to many in today's
Body of Messiah: "All I have is a handful of meal, a little
oil, and a couple of lousy sticks. I'm as good as dead."
Too many of us feel as if we are constantly living on the

brink of death—that this is our lot in life, should we happen to live another day at all.

Perhaps we can learn from the lesson Eliyahu taught this hopeless widow. Eliyahu saw that the widow was full of fear, and what little faith she did have was in her own strength rather than in the One who could truly provide for her. So Eliyahu put a challenge before her: take the miniscule amount of food she had, make a small loaf of bread out of it—and give it *all* to him.

Eliyahu teaches us a critical principal for living in Messiah: *giving out of our lack builds faith.* Had the widow chosen not to honor Eliyahu's request—had she hoarded what little she had—surely, she and her family would have starved to death, thus fulfilling her greatest fear. Instead, she did as the Man of God encouraged her. By glorifying ADONAI, she was blessed—and her household then ate *"[for many] days."*

Today is the day to *"go [and] do"* what the Lord is saying to you. ADONAI wants you to know that your *"jar of meal will not be used up, and the dish of oil will not [be] lacking."* If you will trust in ADONAI—not hoarding the little you have, but freely giving it to Him—He will give you more than just a couple of sticks. You will eat—you and your household—for many, many days...

ADONAI, send Your rain of provision, but first teach me to know that the little I hold in my hand is actually an abundant feast in You. Show me how to trust more deeply in You, that I will be able to respond when I am asked to give. I bless Your Name, ADONAI, for You are the perfect provider—giving me all that I need at exactly the right time. You deserve honor and glory and praise, O God. In You, I have no fear. Thank You for giving me more than enough....

"...How beloved [are] Your dwelling-places, יהוה צְבָאוֹת, *ADONAI Tz'vaot! My soul desires—yes, it has also been consumed—for the courts of ADONAI. My heart and my flesh cry aloud to the living God.... O the happiness of those inhabiting Your House—ever do they praise You.* סֶלָה, *selah. O the happiness of a man whose might is in You—highways [to You] are in their heart.... They go from strength to strength—He appears before God in* צִיּוֹן, *Tziyon."* תְּהִלִּם *T'hillim (Psalms) 84:1-7*

To be consumed with desire for the courts of ADONAI... to cry out in joy with every heartbeat for the living God... to live in the House of ADONAI and praise Him unceasingly forever....

The thought of such enthrallment can be almost too much to bear—the mere mention of it makes some of us go weak at the knees. But on the Day that ADONAI dwells again in Tziyon, weakness will be the furthest feeling from us. The burning passion to be in His presence will lead us into nothing but blessing, pure joy and *strength*.

As we draw closer to the One who is the aim of all our devotion, a hurricane of happiness and joy within us begins to gather strength. It relentlessly seeks an outlet through which to release its mounting, mighty power. No force on earth can withstand it. And as the powerful storm within us finally bursts forth, all fears and weaknesses are dashed upon the rocks. We pour out unending praise to the living God of Yis'rael, and in His presence, we are fulfilled—we *"appear before God"* and *"go from strength to strength."*

Fervor and zeal for the presence of ADONAI is all-consuming—it fills and completes us in a way that nothing else can. In ADONAI's presence, we grasp the reality of what we were made to be—without any verbal explanation, the question of who we are at our very core is answered. When we desperately desire the consuming fire of ADONAI's presence, every area of our lives becomes edified and strengthened.

"O the happiness" that awaits us when we find our might in Him alone, relying solely on Him for our provision, growth, and strength. So let us desire, extol, and cry out for the living God, that we may *"go from strength to strength,"* being ever-filled by the power of His praise....

ॐ ∽

ADONAI, You are God! You are worthy to receive all praise, glory, and honor! I magnify Your Name—I exalt Your Name forever and ever! You alone are Holy—my soul longs for Your great Name to be exalted through all the earth! My heart and flesh cry aloud—I glorify and sanctify the Name of the living God of Yis'rael! ADONAI Tz'vaot, how happy is he who finds his strength in You!

Childish Things

> "When I was a child, I spoke like a
> child, I understood [things] like a child,
> reasoned like a child; but now that I have
> become a man, I have made useless the
> childish things." 1Corinthians 13:11

The Master teaches us that unless we *"turn around
and become as children"* we will not enter the Kingdom
of Heaven. (Matthew 18:3) So why does Paul exhort us
to be finished with *"childish things"*? The answer is
simple: Yeshua is teaching us about being humble and
innocent—Paul is teaching us about maturity.

The plain and obvious truth is that when we were
children, we spoke like, reasoned like, and understood
things *like a child*. As young children, we did not have
fully-developed faculties for speech—we were unable to
pronounce the simplest of words. Even as we grew, we
still lacked the ability to comprehend complex ideas, to
control our emotions, or to foresee the consequences of
our decisions. We cried and fought about things that
we thought were of the utmost importance—though
taking baths and going to bed early no longer seem
quite as objectionable to us as they used to be.

But now that we are grown, we have a choice. We
can continue to act like children, or we can behave as
the adults we truly are. Although we start by setting
aside childish things like tantrums, impatience, and
selfishness, there may still be other areas in which we

need to discipline our "inner child." Perhaps we are overly dependent on other people, or we exhibit the constant need to be mothered (or fathered). Maybe we fail to take responsibility for our own actions, take advantage of other peoples' generosity, refuse to make wise decisions for ourselves… and on and on. But Paul shows us the true path to maturity: *"I have made useless the childish things."*

This is the way the Master would have us approach Him—as the adults we have now become. We will always be children of the Most High, but there is a great difference between being a parent's grown child and being a kindergartener. When we were brand new in the Lord, we spoke like children, understood things like children, and reasoned like children. But now, we are becoming adults in Him. As we grow on to maturity, it is time to be finished with childish things… though we forever remain children at heart….

ॐ ॐ

Abba, Daddy, I am still Your child, but I know that You are waiting for me to grow up. Thank You for maturing me and giving me the tutoring that I need in order to become an effective adult for Your Kingdom. Help me to be humble and innocent before You, O God—but also teach me to be wise and mature, as an adult who has made useless the childish things. I praise You, Father, for You love me like a child, and You are growing me up to behave like Your Son….

"*[אֱלִישָׁע,'Eliysha said,] 'bring me a musician.' And [so] it was, at the playing of the musician, that the hand of ADONAI came upon him, and he said, 'This [is what] ADONAI says, "Dig this valley [full of] ditches—ditches!" For this [is what] ADONAI says, "You will not see wind, nor will you see rain, but the valley will become full of water, and you will drink— you, and your cattle, and your animals."'"* מְלָכִים ב *M'lachiym Beit (2Kings) 3:15-17*

One of the greatest hindrances to living a faith-filled life is failing to make room for God. We often have the mistaken view that just because we have an open place in our hearts and minds, the Lord will give us the faith to change—or the faith to persevere until our situations change. But true faith comes when we walk into the valleys of our lives, and instead of trying to fill them up, we dig until they are full of ditches.

The Lord needs a place for His waters to collect, not to simply wet the ground and run off into some other lake or stream. On the contrary, He wants to *fill* our valleys. Why? So we can drink. He wants to do some massive flood irrigation—to immerse our crops in His deluge, so that we may flourish mightily! And in so doing, not only will we be filled, but there will be enough drinking water for anyone around us—our valleys will quench the thirst of everyone who needs to drink.

Faith is not looking up in the sky, seeing the rain clouds, and then watching the thunderous torrent fill the trenches. No, faith is looking up and seeing a clear, blue sky—but being expectant for the future based on the belief that the valley *will* be filled. *"For this [is what] A*DONAI* says, 'You will not see wind, nor will you see rain, but the valley will become full of water, and you will drink.'"* He is calling us to dig the ditches, and He is promising to fill them—but He will do it in unexpected ways.

ADONAI wants us to be a people who don't need rain in order to have rainfall. He wants us to be a people that will dig ditches to collect rain that will never fall from the sky. ADONAI wants us to know that He will bring water in His own way, in His own time… and all we have to do is respond—respond to the promise by digging ditches, and respond to being filled by taking a long, cool drink.…

ও ক্ত

ADONAI, only You can make a ditch-filled gorge become a valley filled with water. Abba, teach me to not wait until I see the wind and rain to believe in Your Word. Father, send Your rain, and flood the trenches of my valley, that I may drink endlessly of Your living waters. I praise You, ADONAI, for You are the one who sends the wind and rain, yet You can also fill valleys without releasing a single drop from Heaven.…

Until We All Arrive

"... *until we may all arrive at the unity of the faith and of the recognition of the Son of God, to become a mature man, to the measure of stature of the fullness of the Messiah.*" *Ephesians 4:13*

We are on a long journey, but the destination is in sight... and its name is Maturity. For too many of us, however, this is a particularly arduous trip because we are traveling all by ourselves. What's worse, we think that the *reason* we're the only ones on the path is because no one else even knows how to get there! But Maturity is not a place of privacy and isolation. On the contrary, it is when we remain in seclusion that Maturity eludes us. There is only one way that we can hope to reach Maturity, and that is *together*.

Being mature is more than just having a good and well-developed character—in fact, how we behave toward others is a large measure of our maturity. All too often, we remain at arm's length from one another, believing that maturity directs us to rely only upon ourselves as we navigate the course of life. But according to the Scriptures, Maturity is not located in the State of Independence—it is at the center of the Commonwealth of Unity.

We are exhorted to *"arrive at the unity"* not only *"of the faith,"* but also *"of the recognition of the Son of God."* If we are to grow toward maturity, we must first be collectively unified both in our faith and in Who we believe to be the Son of God. Who He is, what He came here to do, what He has accomplished on our behalf— we must recognize these simple truths according to the Scriptures if we have any hope of becoming mature. Many times, we walk alone because we are unable to be unified on these fundamentals. But Maturity is calling us to arrive at that unity if we ever desire *"to become a mature man."*

We will have achieved maturity when we *together* reach *"the measure of stature of the fullness of the Messiah."* If we cannot agree on the facts about Messiah, we have no common goal to which we may aspire. We must fight for the truth, swallow our pride, perhaps even concede defeat—whatever it takes—but we must be *one* in order to be like the One who has called us.

If Maturity is your destination, and you appear to be on the road alone, perhaps it's time to stop for a moment and look around for those who are going the "wrong way." When you find them, who knows? Maybe they took a detour for the same reason… and ran into *you*….

৵ ৬

Yeshua, my Master, I bless Your Name. You alone are perfect—the measure of maturity—so teach me to seek You in fullness. Humble me, Lord, that my pride will not keep me from unity within the Body and from maturing in You. Make me strong in my convictions, ADONAI, but weak in following them through without the strength of others around me. Unite me, Lord, with all who follow in Your ways—that we may be one, and arrive *together*… in maturity….

The Word Applied

> *"For everyone who is [still only] partaking of milk is inexperienced in the Word of righteousness—for he is an infant. Solid food is for [the] mature who, because of the [way they] apply [the Word], are exercising their senses toward the discernment both of good and of evil."*
> עִבְרִים *Iv'riym (Hebrews) 5:13-14*

Last week, Keifa exhorted us to be like *"newborn babies"* and *"desire the Word's pure milk"* (1Ke.2:2). He taught us that we should rely on the Word as our sole source of nourishment. Today, however, we are being exhorted to grow up—to be infants no longer, and to *"apply [the Word]."* The Letter Writer is expressing his parental concern for us—that if we do not start eating solid food, our constitution will never mature, and we will be continually unprepared to digest the realities of life.

We do indeed need to feed upon the Word—it is our life, and without it, we cannot survive. But the *unapplied* Word is for babies—it is insufficient for the growing disciple of Messiah. Nourished by milk alone, an infant will surely grow, though he is helpless and in constant need of care. Eventually, however, he will reach the point where milk is not enough—what once sustained his precious little body will no longer be what he needs to mature and stay alive.

Messianic Mo'adiym Devotional **55**

In the same way, we must receive the Word *and apply it* in our lives if we are to become fully developed disciples of Messiah. *"Solid food is for [the] mature who, because of the [way they] apply [the Word], are exercising their senses toward the discernment of both good and of evil."* As mature believers in Yeshua, we are to *apply* the Word—not be inexperienced in it; we are to exercise our spiritual senses—not allow them to remain infantile and underdeveloped; we are to be discerning of both good and evil—not be immature in our understanding of righteousness and sin.

The difference between inexperience and maturity is not information, but application. If we *learn* all about *"solid food,"* but never actually *eat* it, what benefit will there be? As disciples of Messiah, we are not being exhorted to merely *learn* the Word in deeper and more spiritual ways, but to *apply* it—to put it into practice in our everyday lives.

The Lord does not want us to be inexperienced, but to grow up in regard to the Word. Though we crave the Word like newborn babes, the time has come for us to be unsatisfied… until we have the Word *applied*….

ॐ ॐ

Grow me up, Lord, that I may be mature in the way I live my life for You. Teach me Your ways, ADONAI— not just the words in a book, but how to walk in Your paths each day. I praise You, Father, for You are not content to allow me to feed on milk alone. Thank You, Lord, for showing me how to partake of the solid food that is Your Word applied. I bless Your Name, Holy One, for You teach me how to live in You…

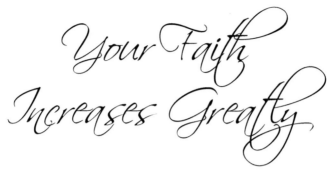

*"We ought to give thanks to God
always for you, brothers, as it is fitting,
because your faith increases greatly, and
the love of each one of you abounds for one
another; so then, we ourselves [give] you
glory in God's congregations for your
endurance and faith in all your
persecutions and tribulations that you
bear…"* 2Thessalonians 1:3-4

The world is coming to an end—the signs can easily be seen. Global tension is ramping up, while national morals continue to degrade. But we as believers in Yeshua are standing firm in our faith, aren't we? We remain steadfast in our outrage over the decline of family values. We continue to dedicate ourselves to attending our religious services, despite the neutral attitude most non-believers have toward us. We stand strong and unyielding, our convictions unshaken. The world around us is going to hell—but here, at a safe distance, our faith does not wane.

Most of us think that our faith is being challenged when others believe differently than we do. But in reality, a disagreement over doctrines and values does not constitute an attack on our faith. Faith is challenged, not when our *ideas* are in jeopardy, but when our very *lives* are at stake. We cannot, therefore, increase our faith by simply burying our noses in a Book. Faith increases when we are *walking out* what we truly believe—when we step out our front doors and allow our faith to confront the darkness.

Faith does not increase in isolation, but when it is tested *"in all your persecutions and tribulations that you bear..."* If our entire service to God consists of being *faithful* in our practices and beliefs, yet we fail to truly put our beliefs into practice, then our faith will have no obstacles to overcome. Whether we're rolling over and taking the abuse of life, or avoiding trouble at all costs—either way, faith does not increase. Faith grows by going toe-to-toe with adversity, and by refusing to back off even in the face of much danger and persecution.

There is glory for us when our *"faith increases greatly,"* because it means that we have remained true to the cause of Messiah. No one will give thanks for us because we are good students of the Word... unless we take what we learn and *impart it* to others. No one will give us glory for believing that Yeshua is Messiah... unless we *shout it* aloud with every fiber of our being. *"Faith increases greatly"* when we put our comfort and security in danger for the Good News—because *that's* when we'll need all the faith we can get....

ॐ ◌

Abba, Father, I can't believe I'm saying it, but I welcome that which will challenge my faith. Put me to the test, ADONAI, that I may increase greatly in faith. Help me to quickly grow away from my timidity. Protect me, Father, as I face the struggles of life—and may the trials I face come about only because of my dedication to You. I bless Your Name, O Holy One, for You alone can refine me and cause my faith to grow...

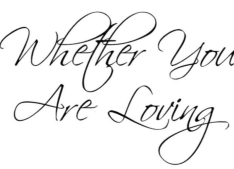

"Do not listen to the words of that prophet [who says, 'Let us go after other gods']… for ADONAI your God is testing you, to know whether you are loving ADONAI your God with all your heart, and with all your soul. After ADONAI your God you [should] walk, and Him you fear, and His commands you keep, and to His voice you hearken, and Him you serve, and to Him you cleave." דְּבָרִים *D'variym (Deuteronomy) 13:3-4*

The voices of our lives are calling us, enticing us, distracting us from the only Voice we are supposed to hear. They are a din in our heads—the shouting of the world, the cries of our flesh. They are an eerie whisper in our ears—the sound of rationalization, the siren of sin. The cries of Self-gratification and Individualism, the wailing of Tolerance and Compromise—these voices come at us from all sides, vying for our attention… and the message they proclaim is the same.

"Let us go after other gods," the voices beckon. Whether from the world around us, or through our own hearts of selfishness and conceit, the voices are making themselves heard. But worse than their volume is the allure of their sound—they feed us, satisfy us, and

tell us what we want to hear. We like to listen because we enjoy the song, and soon we are singing right along. We resonate with the timbre of rebelliousness as we turn a deaf ear to righteous rhythms.

The voice that we love is the one we will hear… and the voice that we hear is the one we will follow. This is why ADONAI tests us *"to know whether [we] are loving ADONAI [our] God with all [our] heart, and with all [our] soul."* We wander astray and follow after other voices and *"gods"* because we love what they are saying to us. But if we will only refuse to listen to their words, and instead give our love to ADONAI our God alone, then *"to His voice [we will] hearken,"* and *"after ADONAI [our] God [will we] walk."*

The voice of the Lord is not one among many, though we make it so when we force Him to compete for our attention. He will not shout above the commotion of our lives in the hopes that we will hear Him. Rather, He will wait patiently for us to decide whose voice we prefer. The voices of life are shouting all around us, while the One voice we *should* hear is getting lost in the noise. Will we lose ourselves in the clamor of their very convincing rhetoric, or will we tune them out completely and listen only to the One we truly love?

ADONAI, I bless Your Name, for You test me to know whether I am loving You or not. Father, I desire to hear Your voice alone, for Yours is the one I love— the One who first loved me. Teach me to walk only according to Your ways, ADONAI, that I may keep Your commands and serve You all of my days. I praise You, Master, for You are calling even when I cannot hear. You are forever faithful to speak until I am finally ready to listen.…

Your Seed Sown

> *"…He who sows sparingly, sparingly also shall reap; and he who sows in blessings, in blessings also shall reap… and God is able to cause all grace to abound to you, that in everything [you will] always have all sufficiency, [that] you may abound to every good work… And may He who is supplying seed to the sower, and bread for food, supply and multiply your seed sown, and increase the fruits of your righteousness."*
> *2Corinthians 9:6, 8, 10*

The seed is in our hands… but for some reason, we don't know what to do with it. Then we remember. "Ah, yes… I'm supposed to sow it, wait a long time, and then reap its fruit to use for making food… But what if it doesn't grow? I'll be so hungry then, and I will have wasted all that seed…. I know! I'll just sow a little bit now and keep the rest for later. That's a good idea. This way, if it grows, I'll have enough food to last for a little while. But if it doesn't, at least I'll still have all this seed! I'm sure I could make a few meals out of that…. Wow. I'm really getting hungry. I hope this works…"

"He who sows sparingly, sparingly also shall reap…" For some strange reason, we feel more secure with a *silo* full of potential food than with a *field* that has already been planted. When God puts that seed in our hand, our first reaction is usually to hoard it away—to keep it

for when we think we're *really* going to need it. But the problem is that if we don't get the seed into the ground, we'll die of starvation before we have a chance to produce any fruit. Unsown seed is as good as if God had given us nothing at all.

But *"God is able to cause all grace to abound to you, that in everything [you will] always have all sufficiency."* We can store the seed that ADONAI has given us and hope that the little we plant will be enough—or we can sow generously with the confidence and faith that *"He who is supplying seed to the sower, and bread for food, [will] supply and multiply [our] seed sown, and increase the fruits of [our] righteousness."*

If we sow our seed without restraint—no matter how small our stock—not only will the seed *sown* be multiplied, but so will our supply. There will always be enough food because there will always be more seed— provided we sow the seed that we have been given. When we fail to sow the seed we have, there can be no increase. But *"He who sows in blessings, in blessings also shall reap..."*

So here we stand before the fields of our life. Will we squirrel away the little we have, or sow abundantly in blessings? The seed is in our hands...

𝜕 𝜕

ADONAI, great God, Supplier of all seed—give me the strength and faith to turn over my hand, that the seed may fall to the ground and become a great harvest in my life. Teach me, Father, not to hoard the little I have, but to give it away freely... because more—much more—is coming. I bless Your Name, for You are faithful to increase what I am faithful to sow. Thank You, ADONAI; let Your grace abound to me as I sow in faith for You...

As Soon As the Crop

"This is the kingdom of God: it is like a man [who] casts seed on the earth. [He] sleeps, and [he] wakes up, and night and day the seed springs up and grows—[though] he does not know how. For by itself the earth brings forth fruit—first the stalk, after that the head, after that the full grain in the head. And as soon as the crop [is ready to] yield itself, immediately the man sends forth the sickle, because the harvest has come." Mark 4:26-29

What proof do we have that the seed *we* scatter is the same seed that sprouts and grows? The evidence is all circumstantial. We reason that since something grows where we have scattered, it has indeed grown from *our* seed. The reality is that we never actually witness the seed from the moment it leaves our hand and is tilled in the ground—we simply trust that what we have planted is what will grow. At night we sleep, during the day we are awake—but how it grows, we just don't know.

"By itself," the Scriptures say, the soil produces a crop—the *"earth brings forth fruit"* of herself. What a mystery! It is not the seed or the sower that produces the crop, but the soil *"by itself,"* with no help from man.

The man's work has already been done: he scattered the seed on the ground. Once embedded in its birthing place, life springs forth—life from the soil of the earth.

"First the stalk," the support structure, planted deep in the life-giving soil. *"After that the head,"* the housing for the fruit of the crop. *"After that the full grain in the head,"* the fruit comes forth in abundance. In perfect time and godly order, life gives way to fullness—the seedling grows to maturity.

From its humble beginnings as a seed in a farmer's hand, the destiny of the seedling is realized—it has reached its fullest potential. But even in its grandest state, it stands there pristine, yet failing to serve its ultimate purpose. It is mature and can grow no more— *"the crop is ready,"* yet it does not live up to its goal. Finally, *"the man sends forth the sickle"*—life gives birth to death. The crop is cut down in its prime, now able to finally fulfill its destiny.

We, like the farmer's seed, have been scattered on the ground—but He is calling us today to sprout and grow. How, we won't know. But by itself, the Spirit produces a crop. The Lord is calling us to lay down our lives, for the time is at hand when the head will be full of grain. And as soon as the crop is ready, He will come with his sickle. Let us yield ourselves, *"because the harvest has come."*

∾ ∾

Lord, God, grow me up to cut me down—mature me to my fullest potential, then take me for Yourself and use me for Your purposes. Abba, I surrender to You, for I cannot know how seeds sprout and grow. Only You, My Creator, can fathom this mystery. I bless your Name, O God, for You are great. Scatter me, God, and give me life; make my crops ready, and come for Your harvest....

*"He who gathers in summer is a wise
son, [but] he who sleeps in harvest [time]
is a son [who] causes shame."*
מִשְׁלֵי *Mish'lei (Proverbs) 10:5*

In a time long forgotten, the people of Yis'rael were
once very aware of the Lord's seasons and appointed
times. It was crucial to watch the sun and the moon
and remain fixed on the heavens—to be certain to know
when to plant, when to wait, when to harvest, and when
to let the land lie fallow. The anticipation between
events was as important as the designated times
themselves. So they submitted to the natural tempo of
the heavenlies to meet God when He said it was time.

We can learn a valuable lesson from this simple
cycle of life. We plant, and then watch and wait for the
harvest to be declared ripe before setting out to gather
the crops. The *"wise son"* is not wise because he stops to
ponder if the correct time for harvesting has come—he
is wise because he *"gathers in summer,"* the appointed
time. The season has arrived—regardless of his
understanding or comprehension—so he responds
wisely, and gathers.

But *"he who sleeps in harvest [time] is a son [who]
causes shame."* We may doze off during the harvest for
any number of reasons—we might be lazy, we might be
sick, perhaps we just think we know better and have
decided that what God is telling us is just not good

enough. But ultimately, we miss the harvest because we aren't vigilant in watching the clock. This is exactly why the sons of Yis'rael were commanded to count from the *omer*—they needed to know where they were on God's schedule, so that they would be ready to reap when it was time.

The reason we have trouble getting our lives to intersect with God's will is simple: we're keeping our *own* schedules. Rather than looking up and fixing our eyes on the Father to stay in synch with what *He's* doing, we usually have our heads buried in our own busy-ness, missing even the most obvious things around us. It's time to wake up and be vigilant, so that the seasons of ADONAI will no longer pass us by. It's time to be *"wise son[s]"* and keep pace with the Father, so that when summer comes, we will be ready to gather the harvest.

↾ ↽

Abba, Father, wake me in time for the harvest—do not let my eyes grow heavy as You call me to rise up. Teach me to stay in tempo with the rhythms You have set in place, and to love Your ways above my own. I do not want to cause shame, O God, but to gather as soon as the crops are ripe. I praise You, Father, for by Your hand, You have set all things in motion—especially seedtime and harvest....

And Yeshua Grew

*"And the child [Yeshua] grew and
became strong… being filled with wisdom,
and the grace of God was upon Him….
And Yeshua was advancing in wisdom,
and in stature, and in favor with God and
men." Luke 2:40, 52*

We know very little about Yeshua's childhood.
Perhaps the Scriptures do not tell us much about it
because there is not much to tell. Of all the little Jewish
boys in 1st century Yis'rael, Yeshua—in all His
humanity—probably lived the simplest of lives. But
from what little the Scriptures do tell us, no matter how
simple or "normal" a childhood He had, Yeshua was far
from "normal" in His experience and substance.

Many times, we look at the standard of Yeshua's life
as an unattainable goal, feeling that we can never
measure up to His example. Yet the Scriptural
descriptions of the young Yeshua ought to give us
confidence. As we pursue holiness, trying to emulate
the Master, we can be encouraged by His humble
beginnings.

Like every healthy child, Yeshua *"grew and became
strong"*—He grew *"in stature."* Simply put, the boy
grew into a man. As He progressed in age, so did He
progress in strength—this is the "usual" process of
things. Perhaps from this we may find hope. If the
Master grew up in the "usual" manner as all people do,

maybe the "*un*usual" wisdom and favor that was upon Him is not so far away for us.

Yeshua deserves all the glory and praise, to be honored above all as King. He is Messiah, the Word come as flesh, in whom the fullness of Deity dwells; and there has never been, nor will there ever be again anyone who is His equal. But in spite of this truth that we profess, we need to ask ourselves some questions. Is Yeshua's humanity merely an icon of the impossible, or are we actually able to walk in His footsteps? Do we really have any hope for living holy and godly lives?

As we grow toward maturity, we are faced with a decision. Will we follow after the Master with a sense of hopelessness that we can never be like Him, or will we follow Him as His students—studying and walking in the ways of the Teacher in the hopes that one day we *will* be like Him? Let us seek to grow, to become strong, to be filled with wisdom, and to gain the favor of both people and God. But most of all, let us believe that we *can* be like the Master—that we, too, can grow in "unusual" ways...

ॐ ✑

Abba, Father, thank You for sending Your Son to walk ahead of me, that I may follow in His footsteps. I praise You, ADONAI, for leading me down the path of wisdom and favor as I humbly follow my Master. I bless Your Name, O God, for in Yeshua, You have not given us an impossible model to copy. Teach me, Father, to live out the fullness of my humanity—to advance, be filled, and grow....

In Your Thinking

> "...*since you are earnestly desirous of spiritual gifts, seek that you may abound for the building up of [those in] the assembly.... Brothers, be not children in your thinking, but in evil, be infants, and in thinking, be mature.*" *1Corinthians 14:12, 20*

In our passion and zeal for God, we run after Him. We seek Him with all our heart, longing to be in His presence. But sometimes in our desire to experience God more tangibly and profoundly, we lose sight of the bigger picture. Like children, we become fixated on the object of our desire—and until we reach it, everyone and everything around us fades into the background. Childlike faith morphs into childish cravings, and we cross a line between wanting more of God and just simply wanting more.

"Brothers, be not children in your thinking, but in evil, be infants..." Children are naturally motivated to fulfill their own wishes above the needs of others, and it is in this way that we become *"children in [our] thinking."* When our zealousness for the things of God surpasses the love and care we should have for our brothers, we drift into the ways of *"evil"* and our passion for God becomes tainted. *"In evil,"* we are instead to *"be infants"*—as we grow up in our thinking, we are to remain innocent and inexperienced in the ways of wickedness.

"In evil, be infants, and in thinking, be mature."
Rather than seeking only to fulfill our own spiritual needs, we need to be concerned with the welfare and building up of our brothers in Messiah. We grow away from childish thinking and maturity in evil when we are even more zealous for our brothers' edification than we are for our own. Maturity in thinking comes not by feeding our own desires—even our desires for God— but by serving the needs of the whole Body.

We must be aware that every passion—no matter how good and holy—can be twisted to serve the cravings of our flesh. As disciples of Messiah, we are not called to follow the Master as isolated individuals— we are members of one Body, working together toward our common goal in Him. Let us run after God with unending passion, but let us do so in the company and strength of the whole Body. Let us no longer be *"children in [our] thinking, but in evil, be infants, and in thinking, be mature."*

ॐ ॐ

ADONAI, my God, I praise You and love to be in Your presence. Show me, Father, where I have been childish in my thinking, so that I may grow and become mature in the way I follow You. Teach me to be zealous for serving others, instead of always being so self-serving. Change my thinking, Lord, that I may no longer be consumed by my selfish passion, but devoted to selflessness and sacrifice for the sake of Your Great Name…

You Will Break Forth

"*Enlarge the place of your tent, and the curtains of your dwelling places, stretch them out. Restrain not—lengthen your cords, and make your pins strong. For right and left you [will] break forth…*"
יְשַׁעְיָהוּ *Y'sha'yahu (Isaiah) 54:2-3a*

It's part of our testimony, our witness to the world: ADONAI pours out His blessings upon those who know Him and follow His ways. The Good News is that His blessings are always abundant and overflowing—He does not hold back when it comes to blessing those who love Him. The *bad* news (if you can call it that) is that His blessings are *so* generous, they can easily overwhelm us if we are not ready to receive them. Maybe this is why we don't always see the blessings of God in our lives—He does not rain them down upon us because we have no place to put them.

The tiny tents of our lives are already bursting at the seams. We barely have enough room for ourselves amidst the stacks and heaps of clutter. Loads of Worry, Fear, and Doubt are piled up everywhere—usually around the boxes marked "Not Quite Ready to Get Rid of This Yet." We trip over unpacked suitcases crammed with Things That We Don't Realize Are More Important To Us Than God, and the walls are lined with shelves stuffed full of Failed Attempts To Find Happiness and Fulfillment On Our Own. No wonder we aren't seeing the blessings! Who has the room for them these days?

But the Lord is exhorting us right now, *"Enlarge the place of your tent, and the curtains of your dwelling places, stretch them out."* He wants us to have the faith to make more room than we know what to do with, so that *He* can fill it up to overflowing. He wants us to stretch out what we already have, with the faith that our tents will no longer get filled up with more of the same junk. He says, *"restrain not"*—don't hold back your great, big faith, and *He* will not hold back His blessings from you.

"Lengthen your cords, and make your pins strong," or the blessings about to come forth will sweep you away! The provision and joy awaiting us is beyond our strength to contain—but if we *"enlarge [our] tent"* with the faith that He will fill it, we ourselves will grow and be strengthened to fulfill all that the Lord has called us to do. He is telling us today to get ready for more than we could have ever dreamed. All we need now is the faith to receive it… because as soon as we are ready, *"right and left [we will] break forth…"*

ॐ ॐ

ADONAI, my God, pour out Your blessings upon me, as I stretch out my faith to receive them. Show me how to restrain myself no longer, so that I can make room in my life only for You. Push out the things that I have been unable to get rid of on my own, so that You alone can fill my life in ways I could never have imagined. I praise You, ADONAI, for the faith to receive Your blessings. I enlarge my tent for You today, my Master—fill it up to overflowing…

"*Does the papyrus grow up without [a] marsh? A reed increase without water? While it is [fresh] in its budding—uncropped—it withers... even before any [green] grass. So* are *the paths of all [who] forget God; and the hope of the profane will perish.*" אִיּוֹב *Iyov (Job) 8:11-13*

We were born to grow. From the moment we leave the womb, our bodies continue to develop—*something* on or in us is constantly maturing and getting older until the day we die. Yet as natural as it is for us to grow, our survival still depends on external sources— things such as food, water, and air. Everything inside our bodies can be working perfectly in and of themselves, but unless our *environment* is compatible with our basic needs, life is fleeting.

"*Does the papyrus grow up without [a] marsh? A reed increase without water?*" Absolutely... but only for a brief flash in time. They spring forth from the ground—fresh, green, and primed with the newness of life. But soon, they find themselves thirsty for lack of water, and—when they have exhausted all the moisture in their unsatisfactory surroundings—they wither and die, their roots reaching out in futility for that one last drop.

So it is when we as disciples of Messiah attempt to flourish and grow in environments that are incompatible with who we are as new creations in Him. Are we still holding on to old fears, or embracing sins from our past? Are we justifying our questionable lifestyles, or hiding them to avoid righteous confrontation? Are we consuming more from the world than we're giving of ourselves toward its deliverance? Is our flesh feasting on our hypocrisy, while our spirit starves and chokes for a breath of fresh air?

"So are *the paths of all [who] forget God; and the hope of the profane will perish."* If we are planted anywhere but in the soil of Messiah's righteousness, we may grow green for a time—but ultimately, we will dry up and pass away. We remain bound to our dubious lifestyles when we uproot and replant ourselves in the flowerbed of forgetfulness. The ground may appear to be rich and fertile in that place, but unless we remember God and return to Him, *"while [we are fresh] in [our] budding— uncropped,"* we will wither.

ॐ ॐ

O my Master, forgive me for my forgetfulness. Uproot me from my flesh and plant me by Your streams of living water. I praise You, ADONAI, for You are willing to receive me anew, to tend to me, and nurse me back to health. Cause me to grow and increase, Lord, that I may be strong and fruitful in You. I bless Your great Name, O God, for You have laid before me the path that leads back to You. Teach me, Father, how to follow…

If You Seek Me

"For this [is what] ADONAI *says to the house of* יִשְׂרָאֵל*, Yis'rael: 'Seek Me, and live…'"* עָמוֹס *Amos 5:4*

Many people look to religion because they want answers—and many eventually become dissatisfied with religion because they do not get the answers they want. Inevitably, they come up with their own personalized form of spirituality to find answers that they can live with. But those who hope to find quick and easy answers in the Messianic faith will be greatly dissatisfied—for faith in the Messiah Yeshua means a life of *seeking*.

The Messianic faith does indeed have many answers—but by design, the more answers we learn, the more questions we have. This is because ADONAI has us in a life-long process of seeking after Him in order to know Him more. By virtue of His majesty, it will take more than a lifetime to know Him. And yet, it is through this process of seeking that we are refined and made pure—that we grow in relationship with the Giver of Life.

Though we may continually be filled with questions, the Lord is not a complete mystery to us. ADONAI *wants* us to seek Him out, to find Him…and then to want Him more, and to seek Him again. In Yeshua, every question is answered and every desire fulfilled, but only when we submit to the process of seeking, finding and seeking again. We are not discouraged by this process because we learn more of the Father each time. As He draws us to Himself, He causes us to pursue Him with greater and ever-increasing zeal.

The Lord says, *"Seek Me, and live."* Many seek and do not find what they are looking for—happiness, fulfillment, spirituality, peace... and the list goes on. But those who seek the God of Yis'rael will not only find *Him*, they will find *life*—abundant life. All the blessings of God are available to His people... and all we have to do to receive them is seek only Him.

❦ ❧

Abba, I want to find You—I will seek You with my whole being. I give You all my praise, ADONAI, for You alone are worth finding. Father, thank You for the promise of life—I continually crave Your wonderful ways, and You do not leave me unsatisfied. You deserve all the glory, Lord, the One who gives life—the One I will always seek....

Bound to Burn?

*"'…a man sowed good seed in his field, and…
his enemy came and sowed tares in the midst of
the wheat… and when the wheat sprouted, and
yielded fruit, then appeared also the tares. And
the [man's] servants… [asked], "Do you, then,
[want us to go] gather up [the tares]?" And he
said, "No, lest—gathering up the tares—you
uproot the wheat with them. Suffer both to grow
together until the harvest, and in the time of the
harvest I will say to the reapers, 'Gather up first
the tares, and bind them in bundles, to burn them,
and the wheat gather up into my storehouse…'"'
[Then Yeshua explained,] 'He who sowed the good
seed is the Son of Man, and the field is the world,
and the good seed, these are the sons of the reign
[of God], and the tares are the sons of the evil one,
and the enemy who sowed them is the Accuser,
and the harvest is the full end of this age…'"*
מַתִּתְיָהוּ *Matit'yahu (Matthew) 13:24-30, 37-39*

As *"sons of the reign [of God],"* the Master has
planted us in *"the field… [of] the world."* Though *"the
sons of the evil one"* are sown all around us, He
nevertheless expects a great harvest from us at *"the full
end of this age."* But should we be concerned that when
the Day comes, rather than being *"gather[ed] up into
[His] storehouse,"* we face the possibility of being
"[bound]… in bundles, to [be] burn[ed]?"

A life of sin or compromise is not always easily
discerned. At least for a while, there are ways to conceal
our dark, private thoughts and backdoor behavior. In

fact, despite outward appearances, it's possible to go on indefinitely hiding our true passions from everyone—including ourselves—until it's too late. But the time will come to separate the wheat from the tares.

Why are the tares not gathered up from the field as soon as they are detected? Is it because their roots are so entangled with the *"good seed"* that uprooting them would also pull up the wheat? Perhaps. Or maybe it's because when they first begin to sprout, the tares so closely resemble the wheat, that it is nearly impossible for us to tell them apart...

Since the tares cannot be gathered up without sacrificing the wheat, we have no choice but to let them grow up in our midst—and in the end, they will be gathered first. The choice we *do* have is how we will live for Messiah now. Will we grow strong and tall today, becoming a useful crop bound for the storehouse tomorrow? Or will we so closely resemble the tares that we are caught up with them when it is time for the harvest?

In that Day, the Master will not be confused—He will easily differentiate between the wheat and the tares. Let us live our lives to yield the fruit worthy of *"sons of the reign [of God],"* so that in the end *we* will not be *"gather[ed] up first"*—surprised by the company with whom we are bound...

Master of the Harvest, thank You for separating me from the tares bound for destruction. Lead me far away from a life of evil, that there will be no mistake where I belong. Teach me, Lord, to bear good fruit for You, that I may be a healthy, useful disciple for Your Kingdom. I praise You, ADONAI, for in You I am not bound to burn, but to yield an abundant bounty for Your great, holy, and wonderful Name....

Borne About By Every Wind

"…may we no longer be babes, tossed [by the sea] and borne about by every wind of teaching, by men's sleight [of hand], by [their] craftiness, into the deception of [their] leading [us] astray…"
Ephesians 4:14

For all the advancements and techno-savvy of our generation, you would think we'd be a little less gullible. With so many resources at our disposal for gathering information, any reasonable person should expect to be able to make rational, informed decisions. And yet, we continue to be taken in. We listen to the talking heads who, despite the fact that they are saying nothing, appear to have a keen insight into the truth. We nod our heads in agreement and fall in line with the rhetoric and slogans, thinking that what we have *heard* is the same as what we *believe*.

Faithful babes in Messiah though we may be, too often we are infants in our discernment. The craftiness of men is not limited to areas of government and politics—it has infiltrated the halls of religion, too. Recognizing this, many of us have turned away from these "kingdoms of men" to pursue the "pure Word of Truth." And yet, there are those who are even more devious, waiting to reveal this "pure Word" to us—to expose the evils of men—as they lead us astray by their own *"sleight [of hand]."*

"…may we no longer be babes, tossed [by the sea] and borne about by every wind of teaching." Every teacher, even the author of a Messianic devotional, is nothing without the trusting ear of his students. It is this trust that deceptive men can exploit—not for the advancement of truth, but for the expansion of their own influence and power. Within *"every wind of teaching"* blows an agenda that affects all who hear. We must, therefore, be mature in our discernment of men before we trust the words of their mouth.

Let us no longer fall prey to *"men's sleight [of hand], by [their] craftiness, into the deception of [their] leading [us] astray."* As we receive instruction from our "teachers," let us hear not only their unrelenting dissertations, but the words they are *not* saying as well. Instead of allowing ourselves to be manipulated by many words, may we see clearly through the smokescreen of deliberate ambiguity. Let us be mature, allowing trustworthy teachers to impart the Word of life to us. And *"may we no longer be babes,"* as we begin to discern the true motivation of those teachers by whose *"sleight [of hand]"* we would otherwise be led astray…

ớ∾ ∾6

ADONAI, my God, protect me from the wolves who would come in to destroy Your flock. Increase my trust for those good teachers who have only my personal welfare at heart… but grow discernment in me, that I may see through the craftiness of men—those who would build a kingdom for themselves. I praise You, ADONAI, for by Your Spirit, You reveal the motivations of men's hearts. Mature me, Lord, that I may no longer be naïve, and help me to trust only those who love You and me more than they love themselves…

"Sow for yourselves in righteousness,
reap according to loving-kindness, break up
the fallow ground for yourselves, [because it
is] time to seek ADONAI, until He comes
and rains righteousness upon you. You
have plowed wickedness, perversity you
have reaped. You have eaten the fruit of
lying, for you have trusted in your [own]
way, in the abundance of your might."
הוֹשֵׁעַ *Hoshea (Hosea) 10:12-13*

What kind of farmer plants in fallow ground? Is he
wicked and evil? Is he corrupt and full of sin?
Possibly… but that's not why he sows untilled soil.
Could it be that he is lazy? Or maybe he's just not a
very clever farmer. Perhaps he has simply gone mad. It
may very well be a mixture of all of the above—but in
the end, a farmer who fails to break up the fallow
ground has lost more than his sanity… he's lost his way.

Untilled ground can be deceiving. It can be soft and
moist at the surface, giving the illusion that the ground
is ready for planting. The seed may be sown at a healthy
distance from the surface—not too deep, and not too
shallow—and for a time, it may even appear that the
planting has been a success. But in time, the devastating
future of the crop becomes apparent. In the hard and

unbroken ground beneath, the seedlings have nowhere to stretch out their roots, and the crop soon finds itself threatened by other plants and invaders that have been lying in wait to take advantage of the helpless land.

When we leave our fields untilled, they are quickly overrun. Wild, unwanted weeds that thrive in the shallow soil will soon slither along the surface and choke out the life of our crops. The rootless seedlings will burn up and be destroyed, having no way to drink from the cool moisture hidden deep within the ground. Upon such land, we can plow only *"wickedness,"* reaping nothing but *"perversity"*—all because we failed to till the ground and instead *"trusted in [our own] way, in the abundance of [our] might."*

As we stand before the planting-fields of life, we have a choice: to plant in futility in the unbroken, unyielding, unpromising soil; or to break up the fallow ground in our lives—to dig in, lift it up, turn it over, and then do it again… and do it deep. Only then will we become a field ready to receive the implantation of righteousness and abundantly yield the fruits of grace. Today, *"break up the fallow ground for yourselves, [because it is] time to seek ADONAI, until He comes and rains righteousness upon you."*

❧ ❧

Rain on me, ADONAI, and shower the fallow ground of my life. Teach me how to break up the untilled soil of my stubborn ways, and to seek You unceasingly until You come and rain down Your righteousness upon me. I bless You, Father, for Your goodness and loving-kindness. Plant Your righteous ways deep inside of me, that I may bear fruit worthy of Your Name. Break me, Lord—lift me up, turn me over, and then do it again… and do it deep…

*"Having been declared righteous,
then, by faith, we have peace toward God
through our Master Yeshua the Messiah,
through whom also we have the access by
the faith into this grace in which we stand,
and we boast on the hope of the glory of
God. And not only so, but we also boast in
our troubles, knowing that the troubles
work endurance; and the endurance,
character; and the character, hope; and the
hope does not make [us] ashamed, because
the love of God has been poured forth in
our hearts through the* רוּחַ הַקֹּדֶשׁ*, Ruach
haKodesh that has been given to us."*
Romans 5:1-5

"Let us boast in our troubles! Rejoice, for troubles
have come!!!" If ever there were an unnatural reaction
to trials and tribulations, this would be it. Nevertheless,
we count it for joy when hard times come, because we
know that in the end, our hope will only be increased.

When we find ourselves in times of trouble, we
must remember *why* we are being tested. It's not to
help the Lord determine our level of growth and
maturity in Him—He already knows our status very

well. No, times of trouble are an indicator to *us* of how we are progressing.

The key to arriving victoriously on the other side of trouble is the manner of our endurance. When we go through troubled times, we are given a choice of *how* to endure. Will we simply withstand the pain and agony, moaning and groaning for a season and begging for relief, or will we *persevere* in our endurance? Will we *press on* toward the goal and *press in* closer to God?

As we allow our times of trouble to work endurance within us, we will soon see a change in our spiritual maturity—that is, our character. Without endurance, our troubles do not yield character... only more troubles. But as we persevere in faith, trusting in ADONAI more and more, we find that He is using the trials to smooth away our rough edges and make us more like Him. In this realization, *hope* springs forth.

And this hope does not let us down! It does not *"make [us] ashamed,"* because it is not a *false* hope. The hope that comes from spiritual maturity is trustworthy and true, because we have already witnessed His faithful hand in our lives as we endured past seasons of suffering, hardship and pain. So, let us rejoice, for *"the love of God has been poured forth"* upon us—especially in our times of trouble.

గ్ర ఌ

Abba Father, I boast in You! I praise You because You are ever-present in times of trouble. Lord, thank You for helping me to endure, persevere and trust in You, so that as I grow through my trials, I will become a person of character and maturity. As I endure the troubles of life, make me grow and cause hope to spring forth within me. Only You, Master, are my hope and my shield—in You alone do I boast and rejoice....

More and More Power

> "But שָׁאוּל, Shaul was still [being]
> filled with more and more power, and he
> was stirring up הַיְּהוּדִים, haY'hudiym (the
> Jews) dwelling in דַּמֶּשֶׂק, Damesek,
> proving that this [Yeshua] is the
> Messiah." Acts 9:22

Why does God grow us to maturity? Is it so that we
will be happier or more satisfied in life? Does He do it
so that we will be more holy or better able to keep His
commands? Is maturity the ultimate goal of becoming
mature? No, ADONAI needs a vessel of maturity so that
He can fill it *"with more and more power."* Only then
will our living testimony be a reliable witness to the
reality that *"[Yeshua] is the Messiah."*

Because Shaul was *"[being] filled with more and
more power,"* he was *"stirring up"* the Y'hudiym. Power
from God is visible and demonstrative, and it flows
contrary to the ways of the world. ADONAI's power is
disruptive, causing the steady flow of soul-numbing
worldliness to stop short and disperse. When we are
filled with God's power, a circle of confusion is created
around us—not within us—since the confounding
spirits of this world are thrown into disorder.

When we operate with power, we become like the eye of a storm. Pandemonium is created all around us, but at the center, there is peace and tranquility. The eye of the storm is where people find the proof that Yeshua is the Messiah, as the power of God reveals Him to those trapped in a whirlwind of confusion.

ADONAI wants to grow us to maturity so that He can continually fill us with more and more power. The more we submit and humble ourselves in all circumstances, the more we will be filled, and the greater the testimony will be. He is calling us to stir things up, to disrupt the blindness of the world around us. So let us not be satisfied with personal growth alone, but let us cry out for the power of ADONAI in our lives—that we may cause a great commotion, and prove that Yeshua is the Messiah.

ತಿ ೀ

ADONAI, fill me with more and more power. Grow me, so that I may be used as a vessel worthy of Your greatness. Abba, thank You for this time of growing and maturity—I stand in awe of Your wisdom and Your majesty. Use me to prove that Yeshua is the Messiah by demonstrating Your power through me. I yield and submit, God of Strength and Might, to Your awesome, powerful ways....

"From my distress I called יָהּ, Yah— יָהּ, Yah answered [and set] me in an expansive place." תְּהִלִּם *T'hillim (Psalms) 118:5*

"O Lord, where are You? The enemy is all around! I don't know where to go… I have nowhere else to turn." As we persevere through difficult and trying times, it is not uncommon to begin feeling closed in— spiritually and emotionally claustrophobic. When this happens, it's easy to lose sight of where we're headed as we are consumed by the struggle. Soon, we forget where we were trying to go in the first place, and become so engrossed in the battle that it is all we can see.

The enemy's strategy is to lead us into a perpetual loop of confusion, keeping us unaware of our ability to move forward. Unable to see the Goal, we stumble about aimlessly and accomplish nothing. Our only hope of overcoming this tactic is to keep our eyes on the Lord—to keep Him in such focus that if we lose sight even for an instant, our immediate instinct will be to locate Him again at all costs. We must train ourselves to keep our spiritual wits about us, so that we will be able to regain our bearings in the most trying of times.

"*From my distress I called* יָהּ, *Yah…*" If we have lost sight of the Goal, we will not find Him by way of map and compass. We must call out by faith, not knowing from which direction He will respond. Then we wait, ready to move when we hear His voice. Not only does He answer, but He brings relief and shows us the way: "יָהּ, *Yah answered [and set] me in an expansive place.*" The walls move back, the pressure is released, the confusion dissipates, and we are given room to breathe.

The Lord does not leave us to struggle alone. It is His desire to give us more room—to give us a way out when there is nowhere else to go. As we persevere through times of great distress, we must remember above all else to call His Name, for only then will we be able to keep going when we have run out of room. When we call out to ADONAI, He will always give light to the path and make it broader under our feet. In our distress, let us not forget to call Yah, because victory and rest await us in His "*expansive place…*"

છ ૭

ADONAI, help me to keep going. From my distress I call on You, Yah—thank You for setting me in an expansive place and giving me more room. I praise You, ADONAI, for You remove the confusion, and remind me of the power of Your Name—You keep me moving steadily forward as You miraculously expand the space before me. You are worthy of all honor and glory, O Lord, for You always bring relief when I can bear no more. When I call, You are quick to reply, and in Your answer, I am saved….

Pop Quiz

> "*...then Yeshua, having lifted up* His *eyes and having seen that a large crowd was coming to Him, said to Philip, 'Where shall we buy loaves [of bread], that these [people] may eat?'—and He said this [to] test [Philip], for [Yeshua] Himself knew what He was about to do.*" יוֹחָנָן *Yochanan (John) 6:5-6*

Was Yeshua really testing Philip, or was He just messing with Philip's head? It almost seems like the Master was teasing him—goading him into making a mistake. No, the Master knew what Philip was thinking, and like a good teacher, Yeshua saw an opportunity to impart a life-long truth into Philip's heart.

As the large crowd was approaching them, Philip began to feel a little panicky. In fact, in Philip's mind, the inevitable problem of feeding this multitude had already gone far beyond *where* to buy food, but that *"two hundred [days' wages] worth of bread [would] not be sufficient for them."* (v. 7) This makes the exchange between Yeshua and Philip quite telling, for Philip never answered the Master's question—he was responding to the anxiety in his own heart, rather than answering the voice of the Lord.

Andrew, on the other hand, had an interesting take on the situation. He heard Yeshua's question, *"Where shall we buy loaves [of bread]?"* But instead of being concerned about *buying* the bread, Andrew simply concluded that the people needed some food. So Andrew offered up a young man with five loaves of bread and two fish.

What was Andrew thinking? Even though Philip had his issues, he was still technically correct in his assessment: they did not have the resources to feed the multitude. Obviously, Andrew's solution was in error. Or was it?

That day, Yeshua fed a full meal to five thousand souls with only five loaves of bread and some fish.

What is the lesson the Master is teaching us today? We do not need to be able to figure out an answer in order to trust that Yeshua can solve every problem. When there is a need, He doesn't want us to go looking for a solution—He wants us to meet the need! If five thousand people are hungry, give them food. Where all the food will come from is irrelevant—just start giving from what you have, and God will make up the rest.

Today, the Master is testing our knowledge of the Law of Multiplicity: ADONAI + faith = more than enough....

෨ ෬

Abba, teach me to set aside the things I see with my eyes, and help me to trust in Your total provision. Lord, You are the only solution to every problem, and I submit to Your loving ways. I praise You, ADONAI, because to You, a miracle is nothing more than meeting a need. You are worthy of glory, Lord, and I give You all honor and praise. Thank You for testing me, and reminding me that every answer is found in You...

"Righteous are You, O ADONAI, when I plead with You. Yet, I would speak with You [about Your] judgments: Why does the way of the wicked prosper? All [who] deal treacherously [live] at ease. You have planted them; yes, they have taken root. They go on; yes, they bear fruit. You are near in their mouths, but far off from their inmost parts." יִרְמְיָהוּ *Yir'm'yahu* (Jeremiah) 12:1-2

What's the point? Why should I make things harder for myself than they already are? Life is too short to spend it acting righteously—I can cut all kinds of corners and have everything I want. Power, money, and influence… it's all within my grasp. All I have to do is reach out and take it. And the kicker? God's going to bless it. As I deceive others, He is going to cause me to thrive and prosper and be the envy of all those who are suffering for the sake of righteousness. My life will even cause those with flawless integrity to question their own uprightness… and their God.

In our self-righteousness, we approach ADONAI to present our air-tight case: "You've made a mistake, God! The deceitful and faithless are prospering—and that's not right; it's not what You promised. But I can help You out here, being blameless as I am—surely, You should take my counsel in this matter." So, we complain in our jealousy, *kvetch* in our pride, and question the Maker's judgment. The problem is that we're so busy arguing the obvious injustice that we overlook one small detail…

If the wicked can be planted by ADONAI, take root and bear fruit, *how much more* should *we* be prospering as disciples of Messiah… *and what are we doing wrong if we're not?*

Being planted is not the issue—it's *where* we are planted. Taking root is not the point—it's *how* our roots are growing. Bearing fruit is not the goal—it's the *kind* of fruit we bear. As long as we are wasting our time and energy being envious of the prosperity of others, we will fail to tend the fields over which we have been made responsible.

Though they may prosper now, the fields of the wicked will one day be desolate. Where they sow wheat, they will reap thorns; though they wear themselves out with work, they will bear only the shame of an empty harvest. But what are *we* doing to keep from sharing that fate? In our self-righteousness, ADONAI is near to our mouths… but how close is He to our inward parts?

Is it possible that the wicked are prospering because *we're* not out there working the fields? It's time to get to work and give God a good reason to cause *our* crops to prosper…

ॐ ॐ

ADONAI, Judge of the Righteous and the Wicked alike, let me not stumble in my envy, but help me to thrive in the land You have given me. I praise You, Lord, for You plant whom You choose to plant, and Your justice will always prevail. May You not only be close to my mouth, but near to my inmost parts. Help me always to trust Your righteous ways. I bless Your Name, ADONAI, for You have chosen me to work Your fields…

Sack of Seed

*"Those who sow in tears will reap
with cries of joy. He who goes out
weeping, bearing the sack of seed, [will]
surely come in with cries of joy, bearing his
sheaves!"* תְּהִלִּם *T'hillim (Psalms) 126:5-6*

When the future looks grim and we feel as if there is
no hope, our natural inclination is to draw the curtains,
climb into bed, curl up under the blankets, and sleep as
much as we can. All we want is to avoid thinking about
our lives. At our lowest point, our moans of grief turn
to silence. Then we stare at the ceiling and ask, "Why,
Lord? Why?" Though we seek the refuge of sleep, our
nights become restless, and we spiral into depression
and self-pity.

But ADONAI has a plan for turning it around…. All
is not lost! Though we weep and groan, the only way
we will truly be defeated is by doing nothing—by giving
up. Instead, although we *"go out weeping,"* we must
bear our *"sack of seed"* and sow its contents in spite of
our tears. So we heave the bag over one shoulder and
trudge out to the field. Why? Because it is the most
important crop we will ever plant. Written upon the
burlap is but a single word: faith.

"It's too much! This field is too big! I don't have
the strength to sow into this piece of land! The seed…
there is not enough. I will labor in vain—of this I am
sure." As we stand at the edge of the field, we survey the
land through the sting of sweat and tears. But

eventually, the sack slumps to the ground, and we begin to till the soil.

Then we realize that something has happened. "The work is going faster, and my back feels stronger. Look! It is the end of the field, and it hardly took any time at all. I'm finished, and there was exactly enough seed in this one sack to cover the entire field! Wait! What is that? The crop! It is already yielding a harvest! Hal'lu Yah! Hal'lu Yah! My God! You have saved me!"

When we persevere through fear and doubt, we will be overcome by the harvest. Our tears of grief will be exchanged for cries of joy, and soon we will *"come in."* One day, we lift our heavy burden; but the next day, we bear the sheaves of the harvest. The sack of seed has been given to you—now get up, sow, and reap....

 તે ๔

Abba, Father, plant in me the seed of faith—even if it's just enough to get me moving in the right direction! I trust You, ADONAI—You are my provider, and all Your promises are true. Thank You, Father, for Your sack of seed. Teach me, Lord, to sow—especially when the land lies fallow. I praise You, ADONAI, for You are God, and only You can turn tears into joy....

"And I have given them, and the
places around my hill, a blessing, and
caused the rain to come down in its season.
Showers of blessing they are."
יְחֶזְקֵאל *Y'chez'ke-el (Ezekiel) 34:26*

Phoenix, Arizona—the city where I live with my
family—is in the middle of an arid, desert valley. We
have very little humidity and only a negligible annual
rainfall. In fact, it is so hot and dry that sweat
immediately evaporates off the skin—one hardly
realizes that he is actually perspiring quite profusely.
Here in the desert, you need to drink… *a lot*… whether
you *feel* thirsty or not—and I learned this lesson the
hard way on the day we moved to Phoenix.

Within the first hour of lifting and moving heavy
boxes in the 113 degree heat, I suddenly began to
experience heart palpitations, disorientation, and
extreme fatigue. I was out of commission—completely
useless—for the next several hours. As I laid on the
floor, moaning pathetically to my wife that I thought I
was going to *die*, I was amazed by the fact that my
condition had come on so quickly. As it turned out, of
course, I was simply dehydrated, though I never saw it
coming. Not a single bead of sweat formed on my skin,
and I never once felt like I needed a drink.

The presence of ADONAI is like water—though we
desperately need it to survive, it's easy to forget until we
have gone too long without it. As we grow in faith,

laboring for the Kingdom and serving the Lord, all our inner parts are working together correctly—we are operating like a well-tuned machine. But if we go too long without being refreshed by the Spirit—that living water—things become sluggish and start to malfunction… and we wonder why. When we finally shut down altogether, we hardly have the presence of mind to simply grab a glass and take the sip that will get us back on our feet.

ADONAI causes *"the rain to come down in its season,"* but do we have the presence of mind to drink before it is too late? Will we just let the rain fall on our heads, cool us down, and then evaporate into the air? Or will we lift up our eyes, drink, and be filled by *"showers of blessing,"* the Spirit of ADONAI. Without water, we cannot grow—we will surely waste away. As disciples of Messiah, therefore, we need to be aware of when we have gone too long without replenishing our spiritual fluids—and we need to remind ourselves to take a drink, whether we feel thirsty or not.

Indeed, would it not be better to raise our heads to Heaven and drink all day long?

Abba, Father, rain on me. Pour Yourself upon me, that I may drink and be restored. Thank You, ADONAI, for giving me the living water I need to grow during this season—to remain planted in the promises You have given to me. I bless Your Name, for Your waters fill my inmost being. I delight in You, Giver of Life—shower me with Your blessing…

Integrity or Compromise

"You—do not sow your vineyard with two kinds [of seed], lest the full produce of the seed which you sow, and the increase of the vineyard be set apart [and forfeited]."
דְּבָרִים D'variym (Deuteronomy) 22:9

Like the other commands listed with this one, the prohibition against sowing two kinds of seed in the same vineyard is an issue of *integrity*. This is the same reason we are instructed not to plow with an ox and a donkey yoked together, or to wear clothing woven with mixed thread—the integrity is weakened because the two will be constantly fighting and pulling against one another. The results will be uneven, unequal, unreliable, and impure. It is the same principle that Paul teaches when he says, *"Become not unequally yoked with unbelievers…"* (2Co.6:14) We are to be pure, that we may be strong and free from compromise.

The command is rich with meaning—it doesn't stop with the prohibition, but it also gives further instructions in the event it is violated. We need to realize that when we sow two kinds of seed in the same vineyard, *both* crops will grow. The crops of compromised integrity *will* bring forth fruit—but *"the full produce… and the increase… [must] be set apart [and forfeited.]"* There is a great truth here: when we sow in compromise, we have to watch and wait for the impure crop to mature—all the while knowing that we are not to partake of its yield.

But we have to ask ourselves, "Why would anyone violate this command, knowing in advance that the fruit will be defiled?" The violation speaks to our sinful nature, which naturally lacks integrity. Our flesh makes decisions based on the moment, giving no heed to the future. So we sow in compromise, thinking that the ends will surely justify the means, and we fail to see the long-term consequences to our short-lived deeds. We may have the most noble of intentions, but the crops we planted in compromise will unavoidably grow to maturity. Then the error of our ways will be painfully evident as we reap the fruit of the crops, knowing we can never receive their reward.

As we grow toward maturity, there are times when we have no choice but to stand by and painfully watch the crops of compromise grow in our lives. It hurts, because as much as we wanted the fruit when we first sowed those seeds, we now know that the increase must be forfeited when harvest time finally comes. So we have a choice: obey and forfeit our yield, or take the harvest home anyway—and continue to reap impurity every day of our lives. Lay down the yield of your compromised crops today, and bring in the harvest of integrity….

꙰ ꙮ

Lord, make me pure—keep me from compromise, and teach me to not sow my seed where the harvest must be forsaken. Abba, show me what it means to live a life of integrity, that I may be able to refuse the lure of my sinful nature. I praise You, Abba, Father, with clean hands and a pure heart. Thank You for making me new, and for leading me to a brand new vineyard that will only bring forth the fruit of joy…

*"And it will be—if you listen diligently
to my commands which I am commanding
you today: to love ADONAI your God, and
to serve Him with all your heart, and with
all your soul—that I will give the rain of
your land in its season:* יוֹרֶה וּמַלְקוֹשׁ, *Yoreh
uMal'kosh [the fall and spring rains]. And
you will gather your grain, and your new
wine, and your oil, and I will give grass in
your field for your cattle, and you will eat
and be satisfied."* דְּבָרִים *D'variym
(Deuteronomy) 11:13-15*

"Such a deal! But it sounds too good to be true, Sir.
Now, let me get this straight… You are going to give
my land rain, but only at *exactly* the right time. And
not only that, you're saying I can *expect* special, seasonal
rains twice a year so that I will know *exactly* when to
plant and when to harvest? You're telling me that I can
count on *you* to do all this, for me *and* my livestock, and
you're *guaranteeing* that there will be plenty of food
with which I will be satisfied. And *all you're asking for
in return* is that I listen to what you say and love you
with all that I am? Such a deal!"

It's not a Torah-tightrope He's asking us to walk—
it's a lifestyle of service and devotion. We just need to
remember that He's the owner of the Land, so we are
obliged to live according to the rules He sets down. In
exchange for life, health and blessing, all He expects
from His people is that we *"listen diligently"* to His
commandments. Though obedience is obligatory, He

does not coerce or force us to give it—and yet, there's nothing fair about the deal whatsoever... we are required to give *much* less than He is.

Our Abba, Father, wants to take care of us. But only half of caring for someone is providing for what they need—the other half is keeping them safe. So, this is the deal: if you want Me to take care of you, then you have to listen to what I say. If you don't listen to Me now, you will inevitably stray from this Land—and I am promising only to provide for you *here*, not *there*. *There*, you will have to fend for yourself. *Here*, I promise you'll have everything you need... and more.

With all the correction and direction a parent gives, it is ultimately up to the child to decide if the instructions were effective enough to keep him from venturing out on his own, unprotected. There is a big difference between a sense of adventure and a heart of rebellion—though we often fail to make the distinction. When we grow to maturity, we have a choice: will we try our hand in a foreign land; or will we recognize the great value of service to ADONAI, and be forever willing to obey and be blessed?

It's a great deal—and, thank God, it's always on the table...

જ ⟋

ADONAI, thank You for sending Your rain in due season, causing my crops and vineyards to produce in great abundance. Father, how can I let my eyes stray elsewhere when You have given me my heart's desire? I praise You, my God, for You care for me with loving-kindness. Search me, Abba, and reveal my true motives to my own heart and mind. I bless You, Father, for You always provide plenty, that I may eat and be forever satisfied...

A Crop Useful

"For [the] land that drinks in the rain often falling upon it, and brings forth crops useful to those because of whom it is also tilled, [it] partakes of blessing from God; but [the] land that produces thorns and thistles: it fails the test and is in danger of being cursed. In the end, it will be burned." עִבְרִים *Iv'riym (Hebrews) 6:7-8*

You are the land. The seeds have been planted, and now it is up to you to grow the crops. You are the land. Imagine that it is your responsibility to *"bring forth crops useful to"* those who till you… yet you cannot control the weather conditions, or even the consistency of your soil—everything is completely out of your hands. Still, you are the land. You have been made to bring forth a crop.

Though you cannot tell the rain when to fall, you must drink in every drop in order to yield your bounty. Only then will you partake of *"blessing from God."* The rain must fall—and when it does, you cannot allow it to run off. It must consistently soak deep into your soil, so that your crops will be able to consume the life-giving moisture. The farmer checks the field every day, waiting for his useful crop that he will harvest in due time. Are you getting enough rain?

But there will be a test, to see if you are only producing *"thorns and thistles."* If you fail the test, you will be burned in the end. What can you do? You are the land. You lie patiently under the skyscape. You control nothing.

But you can pray.

The frequent rains come to water you; they quench your thirst because you have not turned away from the Rain Maker. The rain is the Spirit—and it is only when the Spirit rains upon you frequently that you will be able to bring forth a useful crop. The One who tills us is the Master, Yeshua—and it is a blessing to Him when we yield a good crop. Is there any other choice? Yes... thorns and thistles—but in the end, you will be burned.

Pray for rain, and produce thorns and thistles no more. You have been given everything you need to bring forth that useful crop...

Just make sure you stay wet....

ৰ্চ ৩৯

Creator of all things, pour out Your Spirit upon me—send Your rain, that I may soak up Your living water. I praise You, Father, for You have made the soil that covers me, the rain that waters me, and the sun that feeds me. Grow Your crops in me, ADONAI, and bless the One who owns me. I yield myself to You, that You may yield a useful crop in me....

Not Without Witness

"…in the past generations [God] did let alone all the nations to go on in their ways, though, indeed, He did not leave Himself without witness, [in that He was] doing good: from Heaven [He was] giving rains and fruitful seasons to us, filling our hearts with food and gladness." Acts 14:16-17

Many of us take for granted the simple things in life: a full belly, and a happy heart. But these are the very evidences that declare ADONAI is God. Whether one admits it or not, the fact that we even live and breathe testifies to the Creator and proves that there is none like Him—there never has been, and there never will be again.

Despite the fact that all creation continually proves the nature of ADONAI, at times He has chosen to allow *"all the nations to go on in their ways."* Indeed, if we look around us, it is easy to see the multitudes that the Lord has chosen *not* to impose Himself upon, allowing them to pick their own path. As they go about blindly, they eat the food that ADONAI has provided, and their hearts are filled with joy from the Master—yet credit is not given where credit is due, and the witness of God goes unnoticed.

ADONAI is the doer of *"good."* Yet even we as believers often turn to God primarily when things are not going as we would like. If we cannot praise God for the *"good"* that He does, how will we be able to perceive His nature when our minds are clouded by worry and despair? The well-fed, happy unbeliever cannot see God even when the evidence is right in front of his face. What hope, then, do we have for remembering Him when troubles come our way, if we failed to see Him during better days?

Let us endeavor to give thanks, blessing and praise to our God who is with us even between the *"rains and fruitful seasons"* from Heaven. He is growing us all of our lives—in season and out. Though the evidence may not always be *plain*, it should be very *clear* that He has chosen us to no longer walk according to our own ways. We need to learn that even during the times that the rain does not fall and the crops do not grow, He is there all day long, *"filling our hearts with food and gladness."*

ào øó

I bless You, ADONAI, for You make the rain and grow the crops according to Your own perfect will. I praise You, Father, for You provide all good things to everyone. Thank You, O God, for leaving me evidence of Your greatness everywhere I go—truly, You are God; You alone. I praise You for giving witness to Yourself, testifying for all time of Your greatness. Teach me, Father, to walk only in Your ways, for You are worthy of all blessing, honor, and praise…

This One Thing

*"Brothers, I do not consider myself to
have laid hold [of it], except [this] one
thing: the things behind [I am] indeed
forgetting, and toward the things before
[me I am] stretching forth—to the mark I
pursue for the prize of the high calling of
God in Messiah Yeshua. As many [of
you], therefore, as are mature, let us think
this." Philippians 3:13-15a*

We strive for our spirituality. In the hopes that we
will advance in the kingdom of God, we sometimes feel
the need to pad our spiritual résumés. Perhaps we seek
to demonstrate more power through spiritual
manifestations. Maybe we attempt to portray ourselves
as wise or knowledgeable by espousing our insights
about the Scriptures. Spiritual or ethnic pedigrees;
abilities and gifts; reputations and credentials—we
exploit them in the hopes that our feelings of piety
accurately reflect our spiritual reality. But despite our
best efforts, we fall short in attaining the level of
maturity we desire for ourselves. Why? Because there's
this one thing that we always seem to forget...

Our maturity in Messiah is not measured by what
we accomplish for the Lord, or by how we present
ourselves to other believers. We are not mature because
we can effortlessly quote Scripture, or even because we
can lay hands on the sick and see them healed. We are
not mature by virtue of having believed in Yeshua for

many, many years, nor are we mature simply because we love and worship Him. No... there is this *thing*—this *one thing*—and if we can finally take hold of it, we will be mature: *"Brothers, I do not consider myself to have laid hold [of it], except [this] one thing: the things behind [I am] indeed forgetting, and toward the things before [me I am] stretching forth..."*

We become mature in Messiah when we forget all about our past, and instead stretch forth toward the future. As long as we hold on to our sinful ways—the habits of the flesh, and the paths of compromise—we cannot move forward in Messiah. If we hold fast to our own plans and limit God in the ways *He* chooses to lead us, we cannot press on and pursue *"the prize of the high calling of God in Messiah Yeshua."* To be mature in Messiah is to be dead to our past—last year, last month, last week—and to stretch forth each new day *"toward the things before [us]."*

Regardless of the grounds upon which we boast of our maturity in the Lord, there remains *this one thing:* are we continuing to live with the modified, quasi-spiritual remnants of our past, or are we losing ourselves *daily* to gain new life in Messiah? *"As many [of you], therefore, as are mature,"* let us forget the things behind, and instead, lay hold of *this one thing...*

કે ભ

Father in Heaven, I am stretching out toward You today. My heart's cry is to win the prize of Your high calling. Lord, show me how to turn from myself—to forget about *me*—and to pursue You each day in the newness of life. Teach me who I truly am in You, ADONAI, that I may be mature and grow according to Your ways of wisdom and power. I bless You, my Master, for You eternally give me *this one thing....*

"The righteous flourish as a palm-tree, as a cedar in לְבָנוֹן, *L'vanon he grows. Those planted in the house of ADONAI, in the courts of our God will flourish. Still they bring forth [fruit] in old age, full [of sap] and growing [green] are they. They declare that upright is ADONAI my rock, and there is no perverseness in Him!"*
תְּהִלִּם *T'hillim (Psalms) 92:12-15*

"In the courts of our God," we flourish—the righteous bud, sprout, and blossom in ADONAI's house. In His presence we bloom and grow because *"there is no perverseness in Him"*—we thrive because we are continually nourished in the company of His goodness. Planted like mighty trees, we enjoy the blessings of His abundance—we find long life in His presence, and are cultivated to produce only righteousness all of our days.

So, where is the fruit?

As the righteousness of God in Messiah, is it enough to dwell and grow in the presence of ADONAI? Have we been planted in His courts merely for our own blessing, or does our righteousness have a goal beyond personal uprightness? Are we called only to enter into the presence of the Lord, to drink from His rain, be sustained by His soil, and eternally ripen into old age?

"Still they bring forth [fruit] in old age, full [of sap] and growing [green] are they."

In the strength of maturity, the vitality of our eldership, we are to *"bring forth [fruit]"*—to pass on who we are to a new generation. No, it's not enough to simply keep growing taller and greener, being filled with the vigor of righteousness. Others must benefit from the wisdom and experience we have gained by dwelling in the Master's house.

As we age in the Lord, our tendency is to slow down to soak our tired, weary bones in His presence. The zeal and idealism we had when we were new in Him has become a distant memory of our spiritual youth. Now, all we want is to rest in Him—to find respite from a long life of challenges and trials. But *"in old age"* with the Lord, we have not become brittle and frail. On the contrary, we are more *"full [of sap] and growing [green]"* than ever... and it's time to start acting like it.

The generations are waiting for us to do more than just be planted in ADONAI's presence. No matter how old we are—in life or in the Lord—the time has come to *"bring forth [fruit]."*

ॐ ॐ

ADONAI, my God, how Your presence quenches my thirst and satisfies my hunger! But as I am feasting, Lord, remind me of those who are starving for Your truth. Father, even though I may feel old and weak, show me my reality—that in You, I am full of life, green and strong. Thank You, Abba, for planting me in the house of Your righteousness. Now cause me to bring forth much good fruit, so that Your courts will be filled to overflowing for all generations...

The Farmer Should Be First

*"The laboring farmer should be first
to partake of the fruits [of the harvest]."*
2Timothy 2:6

The laboring farmer toils, working hard in the fields. He has planted and cared for his crops, ensuring their health and growth. Now, in the heat of the day, he puts his sickle to the stalks of standing grain, and they fall to the ground in their fullness, ready for use. With a sheaf set aside for the offering, he heads home at the end of the day, carrying a bushel of the freshly cut harvest with him. From the new grain, bread is prepared for his household, and the farmer anticipates partaking of the fruit of his labor. When the bread is finally ready, he enters the house to receive his bounty... only to find *us* sitting at *his* table, devouring the bread *he* worked so hard to provide.

Why does Messiah tarry? Why isn't the whole earth filled with worshippers of ADONAI? Why do today's believers in Messiah exist only in sub-cultures scattered among the societies in which we dwell? Could it be because only a handful of us are out in the fields— toiling, sweating, and breaking our backs—while the rest of us are kicking back in the cool of the house, biding our time and enjoying the fruits of someone else's labor?

In Messiah, the blessings are bountiful. ADONAI is so good to us that the abundance can barely be contained. But in saving us, He did not put the kingdom of God at our feet—on the contrary, He put our feet squarely in the fields of the world, that we may labor and reap a harvest. As disciples of Messiah, we were not given the *right* to rest on our laurels, but the *privilege* to serve Him with every breath and resource we have been given.

Let someone else give financially? Let someone else pray, or serve, or minister, or lead another to Messiah? Why? So that we can beat them to the dinner table for the feast *they* worked so hard to prepare? No, the right is *ours* to *"be first to partake of the fruits [of the harvest]..."* but only if we have been out laboring and farming the fields.

The blessing of life in Messiah is not only in the *fruit*, but in the *labor*. Let us refuse to be satisfied with consuming the bread from another man's table. May we no longer be first to the *feast*, but first to the *field*— for then we will finally be the ones who deserve to partake first of the fruit.

$$\approx \ll$$

ADONAI, my God, forgive me for being only a consumer and not a farmer of Your fields. Change my heart, Father, so that unless I am giving everything I have, I will be unsatisfied with all that I receive. I praise You, ADONAI, for choosing me to be a laborer for Your kingdom—I am humbled to be in Your presence. I bless Your Name, for You never hold back Your blessings. Teach me the joy of laboring, before I pause to enjoy Your rest...

If a Grain of Wheat

"אָמֵן אָמֵן, *Amen, amen, I say to you, if a grain of wheat falls to the ground and does not die, it abides alone, but if it does die, it will bear much fruit. He who loves his life will lose it, and he who hates his life in this world—to life age-enduring will keep it. If anyone serves me, let him follow me, and where I am, there also my servant will be; and if anyone serves me, the Father will honor him."* יוֹחָנָן *Yochanan (John) 12:24-26*

We are a generation of the undead—alive, but in what form? We are nourished daily by the Word; we drink in the presence of the Spirit. We grow, thrive, and seek to please our Master; we fall to the ground in worship, and humble ourselves before our Maker. We have escaped the clutches of death forever through the atoning sacrifice of the Son… and yet, the life we live is lost, as long as we remain alive.

"If a grain of wheat falls to the ground and does not die, it abides alone…" Has the grain of wheat reached its destiny, standing tall upon the ripened stalk? Has it achieved its goal once it is cut down, bound for the threshing floor? Will it live up to its potential if it falls to the ground unnoticed, just laying there and doing nothing? Like the grain of wheat, we too have a destiny… we will die—one way or another. Whether we are consumed as a morsel of bread or rot as a seed in the field, we cannot go on to fulfill the purpose of our life unless we die. *"…but if it does die, it will bear much fruit."*

As disciples of Messiah, we must be more than fallen grain. The Master teaches us, *"He who loves his life will lose it, and he who hates his life in this world—to life age-enduring will keep it."* If all we have become are mature, beautiful, pristine stalks of wheat, we have failed to fulfill our destiny. Growing and maturing in Messiah is not the goal—it is, and always has been, a means to an end. Our "end," then, is to die—to die to ourselves so that we may live for Messiah—for as we decay in the ground, being tended to by the Master Farmer, our lone, little life will *"bear much fruit."* Only in this death will we live: by giving ourselves away to others, producing a new crop of grain that will soon be ripe for the harvest.

The Master teaches us, *"If anyone serves me, let him follow me, and where I am, there also my servant will be."* As the first to die, the Master Yeshua was also the first to bear fruit—*you.* As we serve the Master, let us accept the invitation to follow and be with Him—to be buried with Him in His death as much as we are raised from the dead in His life. Let us no longer be the undead, following Him, yet *"abid[ing] alone"*—failing to live by not pouring into others the life that was given for us. Let us serve the Master, but not so that *"the Father will honor [us]"*—let us fall to the ground and die, so that we will finally be the generation that *"will bear much fruit..."*

ADONAI, my God—I praise You for giving me life... but save me, Master, from this undead life that I live! Make me useful, Lord, that I will be more than a fallen grain of wheat. Show me how to follow You into death of self, that I may finally live the life I was raised with You to live! I bless Your Name, for You have chosen me to fall to the ground. Now teach me to die so that others may live for You... and they, too, will bear much fruit...

Until It Rains

*"Be patient, then, brothers, until the
coming of the Master; behold, the farmer
awaits the precious fruit of the earth, being
patient for it, until it receives [the fall and
spring] rains—*יוֹרֶה וּמַלְקוֹשׁ, *Yoreh uMal'kosh.
You too, be patient; stabilize your hearts,
because the coming of the Master draws near."*
יַעֲקֹב *Ya'akov (James) 5:7-8*

    Waiting—it's not something most of us do with
much grace and poise. Whether we keep it locked up
inside, or let it loose on unsuspecting bystanders, our
impatience usually finds a way to manifest itself in
unpleasant ways. Indeed, some of us may have been
grappling with our impatience throughout this seven-
week season of counting: "Oy! Enough with the
agricultural metaphors, already! I get it, I get it—I'm
supposed to grow up and be mature in Messiah, but I
have to rely on *Him* to do the work in *His* timing. I
can't do it by myself, but I have to do my part."

    If there is one thing that we should have learned
during this time of counting, it's that we cannot
artificially accelerate the growth of our crops—we
cannot force them to produce out of season. As
maturing farmers, we need to realize that we are
ultimately in control of nothing… and that trying to
impatiently gain that control will only frustrate us,
choke the crops, and prevent them from producing
their yield. This is why we must rely on the Master for

all that He provides—without Him, we are just a bunch of impatient farmers with barren, unfruitful fields.

"… *behold, the farmer awaits the precious fruit of the earth, being patient for it, until it receives [the fall and spring] rains…*" The chief produce of every fruitful vineyard and field for Messiah is *patience*. Though it is tedious work to cultivate such species, the discipline required carries over into every other area of our lives. As we have counted and waited each day of this season, we have been learning to bear the fruit of patience. We must bear such fruit if we are to grow in Messiah, for without it we are impetuous, dissatisfied, and always looking away to a future we can't change… all the while ignoring the present that ADONAI has given us today.

Like the farmer who *"awaits the precious fruit of the earth,"* we, too, have to wait for God to grow *us*. Part of being mature in Messiah is knowing when to put our hand to the plow and work until we drop—but also knowing that once we've done everything we can, all that remains is to wait. Have you been listening to the Master, responding to His call, and doing the work that needs to be done? Then now is the time to walk and work in the fullness of maturity in Messiah. So *"you too, be patient; stabilize your hearts, because the coming of the Master draws near."*

ช‹ ⋗

Abba, thank You for nurturing and growing me during this special time of counting. Every day, I have been reminded of Your provision, Your desire and Your ability to make me new again. I praise You, Abba, Father, for teaching me patience—for giving me the discipline to be still and hear the sound of Your voice. You are worthy of all glory, ADONAI; I yield and submit to Your ways, O Lord. Rain on me, and cause me to bear fruit for You….

"And in the day of the שָׁבֻעוֹת, *Shavuot being fulfilled… there came suddenly out of the heaven a sound as of a bearing, violent breath, and it filled all the House where they were sitting. And there appeared to them tongues—as [if] they were of fire—dividing [and] sitting upon each one of them. And they were all filled with the* רוּחַ הַקֹדֶשׁ, *Ruach haKodesh, and began to speak in other languages, according as the* רוּחַ, *Ruach was giving them to declare….*

"And כֵּיפָא, *Keifa… lifted up his voice and declared…, 'Men, Jews!... this is that which has been spoken through the prophet* יוֹאֵל, *Yoel: "'And it will be in the last days,' says God, 'I will pour out of My* רוּחַ, *Ruach upon all flesh… and I will give wonders in the heaven above, and signs upon the earth beneath… and it shall be, every one—whoever will call upon the name of* ADONAI, *he will be saved.'"'"*
Acts 2:1-4, 14-21*

It had been a season like no other. The beloved Master—our Pesach—was sacrificed… it was so sudden… so violent. We ran away; we scattered— fearing for our lives, we forgot all the words of the Teacher. But then, to our total surprise and absolute joy, God raised up this Yeshua from the dead! Who knew?

As we counted the days and weeks from the *omer* that year, we were also finally learning to count the cost of being disciples of the Master. For forty days He remained with us, speaking about the kingdom of God— cultivating in us the seeds of the Spirit that would soon spring forth and bear much fruit. *"And in the day of the* שָׁבֻעוֹת, *Shavuot being fulfilled,"* everything we had trained and waited for had finally arrived… and we were ready.

This is the story of those who were with Him from the beginning. But there is a question before us today, beloved: "Will this be *our* story as well?" We sit at His feet and hear His words; we witness His miracles and receive His blessings. We learn His ways and consume His instructions; we worship in our hearts and love Him with our souls…

…but do we boldly testify with the words of our mouths that Yeshua is the Messiah, and *"whoever will call upon the name of* ADONAI, *he will be saved"*?

This is the day for which we have been working and waiting all our lives. We have sought God for insight and wisdom; we have plowed the fields of trials and trouble. We have sown the seeds of maturity, and waited patiently for the harvest to come. Now the waiting is over, and— whether we think we're ready or not—ADONAI has poured out from His Spirit upon all flesh. Will we allow the anointing to flow down upon us, that we may finally work the fields we have been remade to reap?

May our days of counting lead to a lifetime of bearing good fruit! May our tongues be set aflame to declare the great things of God!

৵ ৵

ADONAI, my God, pour out from Your Spirit upon me, that I may enter fully into who You have remade me to be! For all my learning and knowledge, I bless You, O Lord—but I would rather Your word be in my mouth, that my tongue may be ablaze to declare the truth of Your kingdom. Thank You for growing me to maturity, Abba… now immerse me in Your Spirit, that You may bring my maturity to its completion—and I may be on fire only for You…

"הַלְלוּ יָהּ, *Hal'lu Yah (Praise Yah)!*
Praise God in His holy place, praise Him in
the expanse of His strength. Praise Him in
His mighty acts, praise Him according to the
abundance of His greatness. Praise Him with
תְּקַע שׁוֹפָר, *teka shofar (the shofar sound),*
praise Him with harp and lyre. Praise Him
with tambourine and dance, praise Him with
stringed instruments and flute. Praise
Him with [the] sound of cymbals, praise Him
with צִלְצְלֵי תְרוּעָה, *tzil'tz'lei t'ruah (loud blasts*
of [the] cymbals). Everything that breathes,
praise יָהּ, *Yah!* הַלְלוּ־יָהּ, *Hal'lu-Yah!"*
תְּהִלִּם *T'hillim (Psalms) 150*

How can you sit and read this devotional? How is it
possible for you to be still? Can you bear to hold back
His praises in silence? Blessings for Him are in your
mouth, about to burst forth! This is the day for
remembering the *"abundance of His greatness," "the*
expanse of His strength," the *"mighty acts"* of Yah! With
the clamor of joy we *"praise God in His holy place,"* and
in glorious splendor, we remember.

With thunderous blasts of sound that ring
throughout the assembly, we remember. With the
percussive, rhythmic beating of our hands and feet, we
remember. With the forceful air from our lungs and
the skillful playing of our fingers, we remember. With
the joyful noise of our souls, we give unceasing glory
and praise with abandon... and we remember.

We remember our Creator, the One who gives us life—and we return every breath to Him in praise. We remember our sin, the way we once used to live—and we exult in the One who bore the penalty in our stead. We remember the sacrifice, the blood of Yeshua the Messiah, who selflessly lost His life so that we might be found. We remember His victory over death and *sh'ol*, and rejoice that we are raised with Him to life— abundant life—triumphant and everlasting!

As we release sounds of praise that stream forth from our entire beings, the reality of salvation shatters the deafening silence of our lives. The decibels of deliverance do not permit us to keep quiet, but implore us to proclaim the redemption and freedom of the Holy One of Yis'rael. To all families, tribes and nations; all mountains, valleys, rivers and seas; to all creatures that move upon the land, beneath the waters, and in the air; to everything that lives and grows and fills the earth, to every single thing that breathes—PRAISE YAH!!!

మ~ ్

Hal'lu Yah! Hal'lu El! ADONAI is strong and mighty, worthy and holy, abundant in greatness, abounding in loving-kindness! Yah is everlasting, His reign is without end—ADONAI is King, He rules with compassion and mercy! Yeshua is our righteousness, our Master, Deliverer, and Redeemer—our Salvation! I shout praises to You, ADONAI; I bless the Name of Yah, for by Your Name I am saved, and in Your praise I remember. I'm on my feet, I am breaking the silence, and with every breath of my being, I praise You... Hal'lu Yah!

His Own Blood

"…*into the first [area of the] tabernacle,
indeed, at all times* הַכֹּהֲנִים, *haCo'haniym (the
priests) go in, performing the services. But into the
second [area], once each year, only* הַכֹּהֵן הַגָּדוֹל,
*haCohen haGadol (the high priest) [enters]—not
without [animal] blood, which he will offer for
himself and the sins [of ignorance] of the people.
…gifts and sacrifices are offered… [but] are not
able, in regard to conscience, to make perfect him
who serves….*

"*But Messiah having come [as]* הַכֹּהֵן הַגָּדוֹל,
*haCohen haGadol of the coming good things,
[entered] through the greater and more perfect
tabernacle not made with hands—that is, not of
this creation—neither through [the] blood of goats
and calves, but through His own blood did [He]
enter in once into the holy places, [and] obtained
age-enduring redemption.* עִבְרִים *Iv'riym
(Hebrews) 9:6-12*

The blood—it's everywhere. Everyplace I look,
blood… and yet, there doesn't seem to be enough. I've
poured it out on the altar; it's covering the holy place; I've
sprinkled it toward the people… but now I'm all out. I
can still see them—*the sins.* They're everywhere, and I
can't seem to cover them all, no matter what I do. Why
isn't this working? What am I doing wrong? If only I
hadn't needed so much for myself….

The self-sacrifice necessary to atone for our sins is
far beyond what any of us are able or willing to do. It

would take every drop—every ounce of blood in our bodies—to cover even our own sins, much less the sins of another. But what good would such atonement be if we lost our lives in the process? ADONAI's justice might be satisfied, but His mercy would go unfulfilled.

On this day, the holiest of all holy days, *haCohen haGadol* is expected to do this very thing—to make atonement for the sins of the people through the shedding of innocent blood. Yet no matter what he does, no matter how much life he can wring from the slaughtered carcass, the flow will eventually stop... and it will never, ever be enough.

And so, the Only One who can *"sympathize with our weaknesses,"* yet is *"apart from sin"* (4:15)—the Messiah Yeshua—He has come! As *"haCohen haGadol of the coming good things,"* He alone could enter *"the greater and more perfect tabernacle... neither through [the] blood of goats and calves, but through His own [innocent] blood."* Atonement has been made, and Messiah has *"obtained age-enduring redemption"* for *us*! Justice is satisfied, and mercy fulfilled—once, and for all.

The blood... it's everywhere. And in Messiah, there will *always* be enough...

છે જ

ADONAI, my King, I humble myself before You on this most holy day. I deny myself—my very existence—because You once denied *Yourself* for me. Yeshua, I bless Your Name, for You have done for me what I could never accomplish for myself. My Master, I worship You; I bow down in humility before You. By myself I am nothing, but in You alone, I have so much more than enough...

"חַג הַסֻכֹּת, *Chag haSukot you will do for seven days, after your in-gathering of your threshing-floor, and of your wine-vat. And you will rejoice in your feast—you, and your son, and your daughter, and your man-servant, and your handmaid, and the* לֵוִי, *Leviy, and the* גֵּר, *ger, and the fatherless, and the widow who* are *within your gates. Seven days you will feast before* ADONAI *your God, in the place which* ADONAI *will choose, for* ADONAI *your God blesses you in all your increase, and in every work of your hands, and you will be only rejoicing."* דְּבָרִים *D'variym (Deuteronomy) 16:13-15*

With the sun beating on our backs, and sweat pouring from our brows, we gather in the last of the season's harvest. We have worked hard this year, reaping more than we've sown—and now we find ourselves at the turn of another year. Our work is complete, and we are finally free to rest from all our labor. There's just *one more thing* we have left to do…

Rejoice, rejoice, rejoice!!!

For those who see the Scriptures as one long list of ADONAI's legalistic "do's" and "don'ts," I give you *Chag haSukot!* Not to disappoint, *Sukot* does have its fair share of explicit commands, and they are as burdensome and troublesome as any could be: *"for seven days… you will rejoice in your feast… you will feast before* ADONAI *your God.*" That's right—seven full days of feasting and rejoicing in the presence of the Holy One, at the place of His choosing. Such an oppressive, wrathful, and unapproachable God this ADONAI is!

Though we easily and often become weighed down with the burdens of everyday life, this is the one time of year when we are commanded to throw off our heavy loads and simply *rejoice*! But it is not just any kind of rejoicing that ADONAI commands—it's the kind that goes on and on for *seven full days*. It's a rejoicing that gives us just the smallest glimpse of what it will truly be like when we are in His presence forever.

Why should we rejoice? Why should we feast like this before the Lord? Because "ADONAI *your God blesses you in all your increase, and in every work of your hands.*" If the fruit of our labors came only by the sweat of our brow, we would be too tired to enjoy any success we might achieve. Instead, we rely on ADONAI, the One who blesses us and gives us increase—and for this reason, we can stop for a week to dwell before the Lord "*only rejoicing.*"

Oh, ADONAI, to be forever in Your presence… Your blessings extend beyond measure! Thank You, Father, for Your abundant provision this year—You always provide more than enough. I praise You, ADONAI, for commanding us to dwell before You this week— rejoicing in the work of our hands, while resting in the works of Yours. Show me Your ways, ADONAI, as I feast before You this week… "*only rejoicing…*"

Cause Me to Live

"And you will take to yourselves... the fruit of beautiful trees, branches of palms, and boughs of thick trees, and willows of a brook, and will rejoice before ADONAI your God seven days.... In סֻכֹּת, sukot you [will] dwell seven days; all who are native-born in יִשְׂרָאֵל, Yis'rael [must] dwell in סֻכֹּת, sukot, so that your generations will know that in סֻכֹּת, sukot I caused the sons of יִשְׂרָאֵל, Yis'rael to dwell when I brought them out of the land of Egypt. I, ADONAI, am your God." וַיִּקְרָא Vayik'ra (Leviticus) 23:40, 42-43

What's a *sukah*?!? Apparently, it depends on who you ask. It's a booth... no, it's a tabernacle.... I know! It's a temporary dwelling. A temporary dwelling? You mean like a hotel? A place where a person can dwell, um... temporarily? Well, that's *part* of it, I suppose—after all, it is only for seven days... But when a *sukah* is defined as a temporary dwelling, it's because the *sukah itself* is temporary—it's not a permanent structure. So, for seven days each year, *"all who are native-born in Yis'rael"* are to live in short-term housing made up of a bunch of tree boughs, branches, and leaves. Sounds cozy, no?

As far as lodging goes, the *sukah* pretty much only does two things: it shelters you (somewhat) from the light and heat of the sun, and it provides a *modicum* of privacy. It *doesn't* provide shelter from extreme wind, rain, heat, dust or sand. It *doesn't* offer any kind of protection from thieves, murderers, or any other type of criminal. By itself, the *sukah* is an all-around ineffectual dwelling for long-term use. And yet, guess how the sons of Yis'rael lived in the wilderness for *forty years*?

Now imagine yourself living in a *sukah* in *your* neighborhood. What's to stop a murderer from coming in and killing you in your sleep? What's to keep you safe in case of tornado, hurricane, or earthquake? Your *sukah's* certainly not going to protect you. So here's the real question: in the four walls of your *permanent* dwelling—the place where you live and call "home"— what's *really* protecting you? Brick, mortar, or wood? A lock on the door? When the powerful forces of the world come against you, will your structure *really* be more reliable than the delicate, flimsy walls of a *sukah*?

"All who are native-born in Yis'rael [must] dwell in sukot, so that your generations will know that in sukot [ADONAI] caused the sons of Yis'rael to dwell..." The *sukah* reminds us that our trust ought not to be in so-called "permanent" structures made with human hands, but in the One who has the power to protect us against all adversities. We dwell in safety, not because we have the security of four, well-constructed walls, but because ADONAI is protecting, providing, and caring for us every day. In the end, even the most reliable shelter is just a *sukah*—one day, it will be gone... but we will have a permanent home with Him forever.

❧ ❧

ADONAI, You alone are my provider and protector—no construction of human hands can keep me safe. I praise You, Lord, for even when there are no walls, You shield me from harm and cause me to live. Teach me, Father, to put my trust only in You, and to remember the power of Your mighty and outstretched arm. I bless You, ADONAI, for placing me in this fragile, faltering *sukah*, that I may truly know Your hand of protection...

The Shade of Shadai

> *"He who dwells in the secret place of*
> עֶלְיוֹן, *El'yon, rests habitually in the*
> *[protective] shade of* שַׁדַּי, *Shadai. He says*
> *of* ADONAI, *'My refuge, and my stronghold,*
> *My God, I trust in Him.' For He delivers*
> *you from the snare of a trapper, [and] from*
> *a deadly plague. With His feathers He*
> *covers you over, and under His wings you*
> *will trust. A shield and surrounding wall is*
> *His truth."* תְּהִלִּם *T'hillim (Psalms) 91:1-4*

"*The secret place of El'yon… [the] shield and surrounding wall [of] His truth…*" It's not a fictional place made up in our minds—these are not colorful metaphors created to lull us into an artificial sense of comfort. And yet, this place of protection is only as real as we allow it to be. If we don't believe that it's there, how can we ever visit? And if we never visit, how can we "*rest [there] habitually*"? It's a real place, all right—we just seem to have a little trouble finding it at times.

Perhaps the problem is that we're looking for the wrong kind of structure. It's a "*secret place,*" so we think it must be camouflaged and difficult to detect against the landscape. It's a "*stronghold,*" so we expect it to be made with some kind of rigid, indestructible material. It is a "*shield,*" so we must not be able to see through it; and it has a "*surrounding wall*" that must be too tall to scale or too wide to get around.

So we wander to and fro, searching for this mammoth compound. As the blazing sun radiates unceasingly and the heat of the day causes us to grow weary and perspire, we search endlessly for that gargantuan shelter of refuge. Finally, spying a meager spot of shadow on the ground, we settle in—fatigued— to cool off and catch our breath for a moment. Worn out, we lie down—and in no time at all, we fall peacefully asleep. But when we awake, we panic in our self-inflicted insecurity, bolting out into the sun again to find the comfort and rest we so desperately seek.

So much for the *"shade of Shadai..."*

Sometimes we make our relationship with *El'yon* so complicated that we miss His provision—even when we're sitting right in the middle of it. *"His truth,"* without any additional fortification, is a *"shield and surrounding wall"* for us. We need only to recognize it and rest in the shadow of His Word, for then we will find all the shelter and comfort we need. Let us say of ADONAI, *"My refuge, and my stronghold, My God, I trust in Him,"* as we strive not for an impenetrable fortress, but *"rest habitually in the [protective] shade of Shadai."*

ॐ ॐ

El'yon, my mighty fortress; *Shadai,* my shield and strength—in Your shade I find complete rest, and in Your shadow I am kept safe. I bless Your Name, ADONAI, for I do not need to run hopelessly after You. Teach me to find peace in the serenity of Your covering, and to trust that even Your lowest wall is higher than anyone can ever climb. I rest in Your shade, *Shadai*— Almighty One, my God Most High...

"*Therefore, brothers, be all the more diligent to make your calling and selection firm, for [by] doing these things, you will never stumble... Therefore, I will not be careless to remind you always concerning these things, though [you] already know them and have been established in the present truth. And I think [it is] right, as long as I am in this [earthly] dwelling, to stir you up in reminding you, knowing that soon is the laying aside of my [earthly] dwelling, even as also our Master Yeshua Messiah made plain to me.*"
כֵּיפָא ב *Keifa Beit (2Peter) 1:10-14*

Remember the time in our lives when we couldn't get enough of the Word? We had *several* copies of the Scriptures, but *one* was our favorite. We still have it somewhere, right? It's well-worn, some of the pages are torn, there are handwritten notes in the margins, and meaningful passages are highlighted in all the colors of the rainbow... Maybe we made it all the way through from beginning to end once or twice... Perhaps we even started to think that we knew a thing or two...

And then we decided to start reading other books—*not* the Scriptures, but *about* the Scriptures. We read one, then another—perhaps a *Messianic Devotional*—and another... all so that the knowledge of the Word would be continually reaffirmed in our minds. Books, videos, CDs, the pulpit—one way or another, we're constantly having some form of the Word being pounded into our tiny, little brains, inching us closer to a fuller understanding of God. *So what's our problem?*

Why do we seem to have such a hard time getting the Word from our head to our hands? When will we start *doing* the Word as much as we're *knowing* it?

"Therefore, brothers... concerning these things, though [you] already know them and have been established in the present truth... [it is] right, as long as I am in this [earthly] dwelling, to stir you up in reminding you..." We can know how to live a life for Messiah, and we can be convinced of the truth, but if we are not *"diligent to make [our] calling and selection firm"* by putting our faith into action, it will be as if we have forgotten everything we ever knew.

Time is short, and soon we will all be *"laying aside [our earthly] dwelling[s]."* Knowing the truth is not enough—we have to remember it and *use* it while we still can. The Feast of Ingathering will soon come to an end, and this *"sukah"* in which we now dwell will not stand forever. So while we abide in our *"[earthly] dwelling[s],"* let us diligently secure our calling and selection by acting upon the things we know—the truth that will bring in a harvest. *"Therefore, I will not be careless to remind you always concerning these things... for [by] doing these things, you will never stumble..."*

ॐ ॐ

ADONAI, God of Heaven and Earth, how I long to lay aside this temporary *sukah* in which I dwell. And yet, I pray that You will not allow me to be complacent with my knowledge of You—idly waiting for You to take me home—but that You will instead cause me to diligently reap a harvest for You while there is still time. Shake me and remind me of the urgency for this generation, that I will not stumble in my own contentment. Master, teach me to by uncompromising in my walk and work for You. Remind me of the truth I know... and then stir me up...

Temporary Dwellings

*"And the Word became flesh, and dwelt
among us, and we beheld His glory, glory as of
the one and only of a father, full of grace and
truth."* יוֹחָנָן *Yochanan (John) 1:14*

On an ordinary day, our dwellings—our homes—
are little more than the backdrop of our lives. When we
wake up in the morning, it's no surprise that we're in
our bedrooms, just a few steps away from the amenities
and conveniences to which we have grown so
accustomed. We go about our days, hardly noticing
the four walls that keep us separated and protected from
the elements just outside our doors.

But life in the *sukah*… Ah! There's nothing
ordinary about that! You rise each morning with the
break of dawn, pleasantly shocked by the sensation and
aroma of the morning air. Awakened by the sun's first
rays, you hear the birds begin to sing as the earth
seemingly springs to life. Yet it is the *sukah* itself that
makes the biggest impression, as you realize just how
truly vulnerable you've been. The moment you open
your eyes, you are immediately aware that this structure
hardly provides any reasonable protection or peace of
mind.

And that's when you begin to comprehend the
"grace and truth" of our God. By sending Yeshua to
"[dwell] among us," He has given us provision and
protection far beyond that of any fortress a man could

ever build. In the fragility of the flesh, the Master lived *and died* for us—all so that He could live again in strength and power, caring for us in ways that brick and mortar never could.

Like the *sukah*, the flesh is delicate, weak and temporary. It was in this form that the Word came, showing us that even though we live in this vulnerable and helpless state, there is One who is protecting and providing for us in ways that we could never see or imagine. Yeshua *"dwelt among us, and we beheld His glory"*—an amazing truth which we vividly see as *we* dwell in *His* presence… in the pleasing shade of our temporary dwellings.

かな

Father, I am helpless. Whether I'm living in my house or sitting in my *sukah*, there is nothing that can truly protect me from the dangers of this world—nothing, that is, but You. Abba, my life is completely in Your hands, and I know that there is nothing temporary about how You dwell in me. I praise and rejoice in You, ADONAI, for it is by the glory of Your Son that I am able to receive Your everlasting provision….

And He Will Dwell

"*And I heard a great voice out of the heaven, saying, 'Behold, the tabernacle of God is with men, and He will dwell with them, and they shall be His peoples, and God Himself will be with them—their God…'*" *Revelation 21:3*

In just a couple of days, our time of rejoicing will conclude for another year, and our beautiful *sukot* will be disassembled. This is the nature of the *sukah*—though it makes a lasting impression in our memories and thoughts, it is, nonetheless, merely a temporary abode. The *sukah* goes up, and a week later it comes down. We enjoy the Feast in spite of the inevitability that it must end.

But a Day is coming when all the earth will behold "*the tabernacle of God*" who will be "*with men, and He will dwell with them*" forever! The *sukot* in which we abide for seven days each year are but shadows of the permanent dwelling that God will one day make among us. Our joy will no longer be laced with sadness, because unlike this Feast, ADONAI's Day of dwelling will have no end.

In that Day, ADONAI's desire for His people will finally be fulfilled. He spoke His desire when He gave the Torah to Yis'rael—He spoke it to them continually through the mouths of the prophets. For Yis'rael, ADONAI has long desired one thing: that He would be our God, and we would be His people. That Day is coming soon, when at last, *"they shall be His peoples, and God Himself will be with them—their God..."*

Though for us the Feast is quickly drawing to a close, we will soon celebrate the coming of our God and King, whose glorious reign will *never* end! All heaven and earth will pass away—our temporary dwelling-place in Creation will be gone. But our God will make His permanent home among men, and we will abide forever in the light of His glory. *"God Himself"* will be with us, and He will eternally be *"[our] God..."*

 è ç

ADONAI, I praise Your great and wonderful Name! Tear down the temporary dwellings of my life and come and abide with me forever! I bless You, Father, for the splendor of Your Creation will one day pass away to reveal a glory that no one can possibly imagine. Thank You, my God, for choosing to dwell with Your people— come and reign, My King, the everlasting Light of the World...

If Anyone Thirsts

"*And in the last, the great day of the feast [of Sukot], Yeshua stood and cried [out], saying, 'If anyone thirsts, let him come to Me and drink; he who believes in Me, as the Scripture says, rivers out of his inmost being will flow of living water…'*"
יוֹחָנָן *Yochanan (John) 7:37-38*

"*Hoshiya!*" the people cried. "*Save us now!*" they shouted, praying toward Heaven for rain. Over the years, the last day of the Feast had slowly transformed into a time of magnificent pleading before ADONAI. Even now, Yis'rael still looks to the skies on this day, begging for salvation and crying out to God, "*I beseech Thee, O ADONAI, save, I pray Thee; I beseech Thee, O ADONAI, prosper, I pray Thee. Blessed is He who is coming in the Name of ADONAI…*" (Psalms 118:25-26)

In the midst of the trumpet blasts, the singing, the waving of *lulavs*, the pouring of water, and all the inventions of man designed to entreat Heaven for rain, the Master boldly stood among the throngs of worshippers and cried out to them, saying, "*If anyone thirsts, let him come to Me and drink; he who believes in Me, as the Scripture says, rivers out of his inmost being will flow of living water…*" The people, who moments before had been looking to the skies for rain, suddenly saw before them The Fountain of living water.

All too often, we spend our time looking to Heaven for salvation, when our Deliverer has been standing right there with us all along! Thankfully, He is willing to interrupt even our grand, sacred rituals to get our attention, so that we might see the salvation that Heaven has already given us.

On this *"last, great day of the feast,"* let us stop looking elsewhere for the salvation that is already ours. Let us overflow with rejoicing that whether in times of abundance or times of drought, those who come believing to Yeshua will never thirst again. May we be filled with gratitude that we don't have to put on a show in order to cause ADONAI to hear our cries for help—for indeed, the One *"who is coming"* to us in ADONAI's glorious Name has already triumphantly arrived...

જે ✑

Hoshiya! Blessed is He who is coming in the Name of ADONAI! I praise You, O God, for Your Salvation has come! Thank You, Father, for sending Your Son, the Fountain from whom all may drink and never thirst again. I bless Your glorious Name, for You alone give and hold back rain according to Your will—and yet in all circumstances, by Your mercy and grace, my inmost being now bursts forth with Your river of living water...

Bring It Home

"*And when* שְׁלֹמֹה, *Sh'lomoh finished praying, then the fire came down from the heavens and consumed the burnt-offerings and the sacrifices… and the* כֹּהֲנִים, *co'haniym were not able to go in to the House of* ADONAI, *because the glory of* ADONAI *had filled the House… And all the sons of* יִשְׂרָאֵל, *Yis'rael were looking upon the descending of the fire, and the glory of* ADONAI *on the House, and they bent down—faces to the earth—on the pavement, and worshipped and gave thanks to* ADONAI… *And the king and all the people were sacrificing a sacrifice before* ADONAI… *And* שְׁלֹמֹה, *Sh'lomoh did the feast at that time seven days, and all* יִשְׂרָאֵל, *Yis'rael with him… And they did on* יוֹם הַשְּׁמִינִי, *Yom haSh'miyniy (the Eighth Day)* עֲצֶרֶת, *'Atzaret (assemble), because the dedication of the altar they had done seven days, and the feast seven days. And on the twenty-third day of the seventh month, he sent the people to their tents, rejoicing, and glad in heart, for the goodness that* ADONAI *had done…*" דִּבְרֵי־הַיָּמִים ב
Div'rei-haYamiym Beit (2Chronicles) 7:1-10

We have seen His glory.

He appeared as a blazing fire and consumed our offerings. He descended from the heavens and filled the House of ADONAI. He is pleased with us; we are accepted—we prayed to Heaven, and He replied.

But now the time of celebration is at its end. We have feasted in His presence and been filled with His joy. Soon the King will be sending us home, but today we will rest in the Lord—content in His goodness, consumed by His fire—and then it's back to our tents we will go...

And tomorrow it will be like it never happened...

We have walked with the Master, tasted His freedom, grown in His forgiveness, and dwelt in His presence. Will we now return to our old lives *unchanged*? Will the fire go out, and the glory fade? Will we fall asleep and hibernate until the thaw of spring, just so we can do it all again— and again remain unchanged?

Just because it's time to go home, that doesn't mean things must go back to the way they were. So let us now think about tomorrow. Let us not leave this place empty-handed, but instead bring the fire and the glory with us— that we may be continually consumed... a sacrifice of life.

Today, the altar of our lives has been dedicated before the Master. On this eighth day, let us *[bend] down—faces to the earth—on the pavement, and [worship] and [give] thanks to* ADONAI." Tomorrow, may we be sent to our tents *"rejoicing, and glad in heart, for the goodness that* ADONAI *[has] done..."*

...for we have seen His glory.

૭ન ન૭

ADONAI my God, Your appointed seasons are again complete—only let Your work never be finished in *me*. Master of my life, may Your fire *forever* be in my heart—let Your glory consume me all of my days. I bless Your holy Name, ADONAI, and I bend down before You in worship and thanks. Thank You, Lord, for not letting me go home unchanged, but instead sending me forth... in Your glory... with Your fire...

Glossary

This reverse glossary is alphabetized according to the transliterated English found throughout the devotionals. Each glossary entry includes the Hebrew, transliteration, and English translation or definition. Below is a pronunciation key to assist the reader with verbalization of the English transliterations.

Pronunciation Key			
a = "ah"	e = "eh"	i = "ee"	o = "oh"
u = "oo"	ch = guttural sound in back of throat, as in "Bach" or "loch," not "ch" as in "much"		

יהוה	ADONAI	The "Sacred Name" of God, YHVH, represented by the substitution "Adonai" in all capital letters. (See Introduction for more information.)
אֲדֹנָי	Adonai	Lord, Master
א	alef	First; first letter of the Hebrew Alphabet
אָמֵן	amen	Truly, so be it
עָמוֹס	Amos	Amos
עֲצֶרֶת	'atzaret	assembly
עֲבֹדָה	'avodah	service, work

אַבְרָהָם	Av'raham	Abraham
בּ	beit	Second; second letter of the Hebrew alphabet
חַג	chag	feast
חָמֵץ	chametz	anything leavened
כֹּהֲנִים	co'haniym	plural for *cohen*
כֹּהֵן	cohen	priest
דַּמֶּשֶׂק	Damesek	Damascus
דָּבָר	davar	word
דְּבָרַי	div'rei	my word(s)
דְּבָרִים	d'variym	plural of *davar*; the second word in the book of Deuteronomy
אֵלִיָּהוּ	Eliyahu	Elijah
אֱלִישָׁע	'Eliysha	Elisha
עֶלְיוֹן	El'yon	High; (The) Most High
גָּדוֹל	gadol	high, big
גֵּר	ger	a Gentile who sojourns with the people of Israel (as opposed to a foreigner)
גִּדְעוֹן	Gid'on	Gideon
הַ	ha	"the," when it precedes another word
הַלְלוּ אֵל	hal'lu El	Praise God
הַלְלוּ יָהּ	hal'lu Yah	hallelujah, Praise Yah
הוֹשֵׁעַ	Hoshea	Hosea
הוֹשִׁיעַ	hoshiya	save
עִבְרִים	Iv'riym	Hebrews
אִיּוֹב	Iyov	Job
כֵּיפָא	Keifa	Cephas / Peter
כִּנֶּרֶת	Kineret	Gennesaret, that is, the Sea of Galilee
לֵוִי	Leviy	Levite
לְבָנוֹן	L'vanon	Lebanon

מְלָכִים	M'lachiym	Kings
מָשִׁיחַ	Mashiyach	Messiah, meaning, "anointed one." In Greek, Χριστός, *Christos* (Christ)
מַתִּתְיָהוּ	Matit'yahu	Matthew
מַצָּה	matzah	unleavened bread
מִדְיָן	Mid'yan	Midian
מִשְׁלֵי	Mish'lei	Proverbs
מִצְרַיִם	Mitz'rayim	Egypt, Egyptians
מֹשֶׁה	Moshe	Moses
עֹמֶר	omer	sheaf
פֶּסַח	Pesach	Passover
רוּחַ	ruach	spirit
רוּחַ הַקֹּדֶשׁ	Ruach haKodesh	The Holy Spirit
שַׁבָּת	Shabbat	Sabbath
שַׁדַּי	Shadai	Almighty
שָׁאוּל	Shaul	Saul; also the apostle Paul's Hebrew name
שָׁבוּעַ	shavua	"week," i.e. seven days
שָׁבֻעוֹת	shavuot	plural for *shavua*; also a pilgrim feast
שְׁלֹמֹה	Sh'lomoh	Solomon
שְׁמִינִי	sh'miyniy	"eighth"
שְׁמוֹת	sh'mot	"names"—the second word of the book of Exodus
שְׁמוּאֵל	Sh'muel	Samuel
שׁוֹפָר	shofar	"trumpet," ram's horn
שֹׁפְטִים	Shof'tiym	Judges
סֶלָה	selah	to lift up, exalt; possibly a musical term indicating a, pause or interruption

סֻכָּה	sukah	tabernacle, booth, temporary shelter/dwelling
סֻכּת	sukot	plural of *sukah*; also a pilgrim feast
תֶּקַע	teka	sound (of a shofar)
תְּהִלִּם	T'hillim	Psalms
תּוֹרָה	Torah	Instruction, teaching, referring to the five books of Moses. Translated incorrectly as "Law."
תְּרוּעָה	t'ruah	loud blasts (of sound)
צִלְצְלֵי	tzil'tz'lei	cymbals
צִיּוֹן	Tziyon	Zion
צְבָאוֹת	Tz'vaot	armies, hosts
וַיִּקְרָא	vayik'ra	"and he called"—first phrase of Leviticus
יַעֲקֹב	Ya'akov	Jacob, James
יָהּ	Yah	Jah; shortened form of the "Sacred Name"
יָמִים	yamiym	plural for *yom*
יְחֶזְקֵאל	Y'chez'ke-el	Ezekiel
יֵשׁוּעַ	Yeshua	salvation
יְהוּדָה	Y'hudah	Judah
יְהוּדִים	Y'hudiym	plural for *Y'hudah*— "Jews," people of Judah
יִרְמְיָהוּ	Yir'm'yahu	Jeremiah
יִשְׂרָאֵל	Yis'rael	Israel
יוֹחָנָן	Yochanan	John
יוֹאֵל	Yoel	Joel
יוֹם	yom	day
יוֹרֶה וּמַלְקוֹשׁ	Yoreh uMal'kosh	the early and latter rains; the fall and spring rains
יְשַׁעְיָהוּ	Y'sha'yahu	Isaiah
זִכְרוֹן	zik'ron	remembrance

Appendix: The Mo'adiym

The *Messianic Mo'adiym Devotional* has a very narrow focus: Israel's annual feasts, fasts and appointed times as understood from a Messianic Jewish perspective. The following appendix is designed to give you a brief overview of each of the *Mo'adiym*, in addition to explaining our perspective of these various events. Regardless of your present knowledge of and experience with the calendar of Israel, we encourage you to read through this section before beginning the devotionals themselves.

All of the devotionals contained in this volume are thematic, centering on a particular theme or aspect of a given *moed*—as well as any messianic fulfillment they may find in Yeshua. As such, a certain level of understanding is needed in order to get the most out each devotional. While an exhaustive treatment of the *Mo'adiym* is beyond the scope of this book, we hope that this information will serve as a good foundation for your devotional journey through ADONAI's designated times.

A Brief Word About Jewish Tradition

Who can imagine Rosh Hashanah without the *shofar*? Yom Kippur without "the book of life?" Sukkot without the *lulav*? Passover without the *karpas*?

The traditions and cultures of the Judaisms[1] have developed over the course of many centuries, becoming inseparable from Jewish holiday observances. And yet—despite their beauty, apparent wisdom, and sometimes near-universal acceptance—we as disciples of Messiah have an obligation to at least *reconsider* these traditions in light of Scripture.

With the utmost respect for our Jewish people and regard for our rich cultural heritage, we have nevertheless chosen a "Scripture-first" approach to understanding and keeping the *Mo'adiym*. In so doing, our goal is not to *denigrate* or *exclude* tradition—rather to *elevate Scripture* and allow the *power of the Word* to exercise its authority in our lives.

The following supplementary material therefore treats *Scripture* as the primary source for learning how to practice and understand the *Mo'adiym*. Where deemed appropriate, we also address common misconceptions about the *Mo'adiym* that have a tendency to complicate or make unclear the simple teaching of Scripture. We hope that you will find this to be a fresh, exciting and meaningful approach that helps you to practically and actually enter into the *Mo'adiym*—according to the Spirit, in the fullness of Messiah.

The "Feasts" of the Lord

One of the most common fallacies about the *Mo'adiym* is that they are they collectively called ADONAI's "Feasts" or "Festivals." Several English

---

[1] Beliefs, traditions and culture vary widely among the various branches of Judaism. Since no single sect can definitively claim to represent Judaism, we therefore use the term "Judaisms" to refer to all of these groups as a single unit.

translations of the Scriptures are likely the original culprits promoting this misconception. But as we explore the *Mo'adiym* together, it should become obvious that such terms are not entirely accurate—in fact, at least one *moed* is extremely *un*festive, and there are others that simply have nothing to do with feasting or festivities whatsoever.

The word often translated as "feasts" is מוֹעֲדִים, *Mo'adiym* (pronounced, "moe-ah-deem"), meaning "designated seasons" or "appointed times."[2] וַיִּקְרָא *Vayik'ra* (Leviticus) 23 offers the most exhaustive enumeration of these events in a single passage.

The chapter begins,

> "*And ADONAI spoke to Moshe, saying, 'Speak to the sons of Yis'rael, and you will say to them, "These are [the] appointed times of* (מוֹעֲדֵי, *mo'adei) ADONAI, which you [are to] proclaim; holy convocations. They are My appointed times* (מוֹעֲדָי, *mo'adai)…""'*

The rest of the chapter proceeds to outline the complete cycle of ADONAI's feasts, fasts, and appointed times.[3] We will spend the remainder of the appendix briefly exploring each of them.

---

[2] This word is the plural form of מוֹעֵד, *moed* (pronounced "moe-ed"), and can be found in passages such as בְּרֵאשִׁית *B'reshiyt* (Genesis) 1:14 and נְחֶמְיָה *N'chem'yah* (Nehemiah) 10:34. Another variant of *moed* is מוֹעֲדָי, *mo'adai*, meaning "My designated seasons" or "My appointed times." This is the word used in וַיִּקְרָא *Vayik'ra* (Leviticus) 23, as well as in passages such as עֶזְרָא *Ezra* 3:5 and יְחֶזְקֵאל *Y'chez'ke-el* (Ezekiel) 44:24.
[3] The holidays of *Purim* and *Hanukkah* are not considered *mo'adiym*, hence, they are absent from this book.

Shabbat

The Seventh Day of Every Week
וַיִּקְרָא *Vayik'ra* 23:3

The Shabbat, actually called שַׁבַּת שַׁבָּתוֹן, *Shabbat Shabaton*[4] in this passage, is perhaps the holiest of all the *Mo'adiym* on Israel's calendar.[5] This *moed* occurs more frequently than any other, taking place once every seven days on the last day of each week—the seventh day.

The basic command for the seventh-day Shabbat is quite simple: stop from all forms of work; and rest, rest, rest. Though many people fumble over the questions, "What is work?" and "What is rest?" the answer is seen in the basic contrast between the seventh day and the first six days of the week. Six days are for laboring and doing all our work, and the seventh day is not. It really is that simple—and there is great joy and freedom to be experienced when the seventh-day is set apart in this way.

All too frequently, however, this holy day becomes relegated to a mere "day of worship"—itself often reduced to a religious service, a Torah study, and some food. As a result, our collective observance of the Shabbat can seem to illustrate the old adage, "familiarity breeds contempt." Because we are apparently so familiar with the weekly Shabbat, we tend to view it as somehow less significant than the *annual* appointed times. Not only does this attitude conflict with the clear teaching of Scripture, but it also robs us of a significant meeting-time with ADONAI.

---

[4] Much more than a mere "Sabbath rest," *Shabbat Shabaton* may more accurately be interpreted: "an intermission of / cessation for complete rest"
[5] With the notable exception of *Yom haKipuriym*, the Day of the Atonements

To this end, we have chosen to set apart the Shabbat for its own unique treatment as a devotional source, and are planning a *Messianic Shabbat Devotional*[6] in the future. As such, Shabbat devotionals are noticeably absent from this volume.

Passover

1ˢᵗ Month—14ᵗʰ day, "between the evenings"
וַיִּקְרָא *Vayik'ra* 23:5

Israel's annual calendar of appointed times begins in the Spring with פֶּסַח, *Pesach* (or חַג הַפֶּסַח, *Chag haPasach;* Feast of Passover)—one of the most well-known *mo'adiym*. Contrary to our typical understanding, however, *Pesach* is not actually a *day*, but an *event*—a sacrifice designated for the 14ᵗʰ day of the first month,[7] "between the evenings" (בֵּין הָעַרְבָּיִם, *bein ha-ar'bayim*). This phrase can be interpreted as the interval at the end of the day between sundown and nightfall—in other words, "twilight" or "dusk."

The observance of *Pesach* according to Scripture is very well-developed in שְׁמוֹת, *Sh'mot* (Exodus) 12.[8] Here we learn that *Pesach* is a feast in commemoration of Israel being "passed over" during the final judgment against her former oppressor, Egypt. The elements of the *Pesach* are simple and few: the *Pesach* sacrifice itself—a lamb or goat, one per household; the מַצָּה, *matzah* (unleavened bread);[9] and the מָרֹר, *maror*

---

[6] The *Messianic Shabbat Devotional* is expected to contain devotionals for the New Moon as well.
[7] The first month of Israel's calendar year—also known as אָבִיב, *Aviyv* or נִיסָן, *Niysan*—begins in the springtime. While the Judaisms begin their calendar with *"Rosh Hashanah"* in the fall, this reckoning does not appear to be supported by Scripture.
[8] Other important passages include בְּמִדְבַּר *B'mid'bar* (Numbers) 9 and דְּבָרִים *D'variym* (Deuteronomy) 16.
[9] that is, bread made without yeast or a leavening agent

(bitter herbs).[10] It is also commanded that the *Pesach* be sacrificed and eaten only *"in the place where* ADONAI *will choose to cause His name to dwell"*[11]—in other words, Jerusalem. Thus, the essential commands for keeping the *Pesach* are as follows: the eating of the elements at the designated time, the sacrifice being performed in Jerusalem, and the "passing over" being recounted *"when your sons say to you, 'What is this ceremony that you [are] doing?'"*[12]

Since the *Pesach* story is mirrored and brought to its fullest meaning in the sacrifice of our *Pesach*, the Messiah Yeshua, we should naturally see such spiritual themes as deliverance, redemption, and freedom in this *moed*. As the inaugural *moed*, *Pesach* also sets the tone for the entire spring season of *Mo'adiym*.

The *Pesach* devotional is intended to be read sometime before sundown on the fourteenth of the first month[13] **in preparation for the upcoming event.**

Feast of Unleavened Bread

1ˢᵗ Month—15ᵗʰ day through the 21ˢᵗ day (7 days)
וַיִּקְרָא *Vayik'ra* 23:6-8

Immediately following the *Pesach* sacrifice,

---

[10] In addition to these elements, it seems likely that the Master Yeshua also incorporated "the fruit of the vine" into His remembrance and prophetic fulfillment of the *Pesach*. The remaining items in the traditional Jewish *Seder* are extra-biblical.
[11] *D'variym* 16:2
[12] *Sh'mot* 12:26ff—this and the following verse form the basis for the institution of the Jewish *Seder*, which is simply a memorial of the actual *Pesach* sacrifice ceremony.
[13] All dates given are on Israel's calendar, and will occur on a different date on our Gregorian calendar each year. *Pesach* usually falls in late March or early April.

"In the first month, *on the fourteenth day of the month, in the evening, you will eat* מַצָּה, *matzah until the twenty-first day of the month, at evening… and on the fifteenth day of this month is* חַג הַמַּצּוֹת, *Chag haMatzot to* ADONAI; *[for] seven days, you will eat* מַצָּה, *matzah…"*[14]

The Feast of *Matzah* is a seven-day feast, lasting from the fifteenth day[15] through the twenty-first day of the first month. Additionally, the first and seventh days are each considered מִקְרָא־קֹדֶשׁ, *mik'ra-kodesh*—a holy convocation, or sacred assembly—and include the command to do no regular work.[16]

While *Pesach* celebrates Israel's protection from the judgment against Egypt, the Feast of *Matzah* commemorates the liberation of the people of Israel from their Egyptian captivity. *Matzah*, being a major element in both feasts, ties the two events together, creating a seamless celebration. But unlike *Pesach*, which lasts for a brief moment in time, the Feast of *Matzah* lasts for seven full days! The principal activity of the feast? Eating!—but not just eating in general… eating *matzah*!

We should note, however, that the Feast of *Matzah* is more than just a feast—it is also a *fast*. The instructions of *Sh'mot* 12:19-20 state,

> *"… [for] seven days, leaven is not [to be] found in your houses… do not eat anything leavened—in all your dwellings, you will eat* מַצָּה, *matzah."*

---

[14] *Sh'mot* 12:18; *Vayik'ra* 23:6
[15] beginning with the evening of the fourteenth
[16] The Scriptures do make an exception to "no regular work" on the 1ˢᵗ and 7ᵗʰ days of *Matzah* for cooking (*Sh'mot* 12:16). Rest (שַׁבָּתוֹן, *shabaton*) is *not* commanded.

As one is feasting upon the *matzah*, he is also to be *fasting* anything made with leaven. This can lead to extremely meaningful spiritual themes, including being released from bondage to sin (sin being symbolized by leaven),[17] and then walking deliberately and victoriously in our freedom as new, *unleavened* creations in Messiah.

Like *Pesach*, the Feast of *Matzah* has clear fulfillment in Messiah—Israel's liberation from *Egypt* mirrors our own liberation from *sin*.[18] As we keep the commands and commemorate a watershed event in Israel's history, this feast/fast provides us with a unique opportunity to be daily reminded of our reality in Messiah—that we are "unleavened"—and to deliberately practice *walking without sin*.

The seven devotionals for the Feast of *Matzah* are intended to be read on the fifteenth through the twenty-first days of the first month. We believe the devotionals will be most meaningful if you actually participate in the Feast by intentionally eating *matzah*, and deliberately *not* eating anything leavened (or having anything made with leaven in your home). Though this may seem daunting at first glance, please be encouraged! The Feast of *Matzah* can be a powerful week in your life every year, but it requires advance planning and a lot of grace. Don't allow yourself to feel self-condemned if the week does not go as expected the first time around. If you set your heart *first* on adhering to the *principles* and *spirit* of the Feast, actions and lifestyle changes will follow more easily in the future.

---

[17] e.g. 1Corinthians 5:6ff
[18] Romans 6:18

Counting from the Omer

From the day after the "shabbat," for 49 days
וַיִּקְרָא *Vayik'ra* 23:9-16a

After reading about the Feast of *Matzah* in the narrative of *Vayik'ra* 23, we come to a *moed* without an official name.[19] At this appointed time, the sons of Israel are each commanded to bring an עֹמֶר, *omer* to the priests. An *omer* is simply a sheaf, specifically a bundle of grain from the beginning of the first crop.[20] The priest is then to wave the *omer* before ADONAI as a "wave-offering," so that the *omer*—and the entire harvest as well—will be accepted. Then,

> "...*from the day of your bringing in the*
> עֹמֶר, *omer of the wave-offering... count fifty*
> *days... and you will bring near a new offering*
> *to* ADONAI..."[21]

Beginning with the day of the wave-offering, Israel is to count 49 days, and then on the 50th day—the Feast of *Shavuot*—bring a new offering from the wheat harvest.[22] We can therefore infer that during the time of counting, the wheat crops are continuing to grow and ripen, but will be ready for harvest when the counting is complete. So the counting is a feature of Israel's calendar that instructs her regarding the correct time to

---

[19] Some call this day יוֹם הַבִּכּוּרִים, *Yom haBikuriym*—Day of the First Fruits. However, the present passage of *Vayik'ra* makes no mention of בִּכּוּרִים, *bikuriym*—the word often translated "first fruits" in verse 10 is actually רֵאשִׁית, *reshiyt*, which means "beginning." *B'mid'bar* 28:26 clearly says that *Shavuot*—the *moed* occurring fifty days later—is יוֹם הַבִּכּוּרִים, *Yom haBikuriym*. *Sh'mot* 23:16 and *Vayik'ra* 23:17 also concur that בִּכּוּרִים, *bikuriym*, in this context, is associated with *Shavuot*.
[20] Most likely barley. See *Sh'mot* 9:31 and רוּת *Rut* (Ruth) 1:22
[21] *Vayik'ra* 23:15b-16
[22] *Sh'mot* 34:22

harvest and make an offering from the mature wheat crops.

As we walk through the Spring *Mo'adiym*, we can also see a picture of our own walk with Messiah. At *Pesach*, we are reminded of being set free from sin; then during the Feast of *Matzah*, we have the opportunity to practice walking in our "unleavened-ness." As we count from the *omer*,[23] we are like the wheat crops—growing toward maturity, ultimately destined to become an abundant harvest for ADONAI. During this season of counting, we can focus on certain spiritual themes such as sowing, growing, increase, being fed and nourished by ADONAI, and being mindful of how we are growing toward maturity in Messiah. **The devotionals for counting from the *omer* are obviously to be read each day of the counting.**

Before we go on with the next *moed*, we must note that the day on which the counting should begin is in dispute—and has been since before Yeshua's day. Given the nature of the disagreement, the following explanation may be somewhat confusing.

The dispute hangs on the interpretation of *Vayik'ra* 23:15, which says that the counting is to begin *"from the day after the שַׁבָּת, shabbat."* As a result of three different understandings of this phrase, the time to begin the counting could be the day after the first day of the Feast of *Matzah*,[24] the day after the seventh-day Shabbat

---

[23] Judaism often refers to this time as סְפִירַת הַעֹמֶר, *S'fiyrat haOmer*—"Counting the Omer." This, however, is not entirely accurate, since we are not counting *omers*, but *days*—days *from* the offering of that first *omer*. For the sake of accuracy, brevity and convenience, we have therefore titled this season of counting סְפִירַת מֵעֹמֶר, *S'fiyrat meOmer*—"Counting *from* [the] Omer."
[24] The 16th day of the first month

during the Feast of *Matzah*,[25] or the day after the *last* day of the Feast of *Matzah*.[26]

The current Jewish calendar fixes the date for the wave-offering on the sixteenth day of the first month—the day after the first day of the Feast of *Matzah*. This is because Judaism considers the fifteenth day of the first month to be a Shabbat. Hence, the "day after the shabbat," according to this interpretation, is the sixteenth of the month. According to Scripture, however, neither the first nor the last days of the Feast of *Matzah* are notated within the text as "shabbats"— they are simply designated as days to do no regular work.

Another ancient interpretation—one which has resurfaced lately especially among some Messianics and Christians[27]—is that the "shabbat" being referred to in *Vayik'ra* 23:15 is the seventh-day Shabbat. In context, therefore, the "day after the shabbat" would be interpreted as the day after the seventh-day Shabbat *during* the Feast of *Matzah*. This is an attractive solution for some Messianics and Christians because they believe that during the last year of Yeshua's life on earth, this day coincided with the day of His resurrection.[28]

---

[25] Since the days of the month fall on different days of the week every year, the occurrence of the seventh-day Shabbat during the Feast changes from year to year.

[26] Another possible interpretation is the day after the seventh-day Shabbat *after* the Feast of Matzah, although this view is not in practice today.

[27] and a minor sect of Judaism, the Karaites

[28] Part of the desire some have for finding messianic fulfillment for this *moed* is to validate the celebration of Yeshua's resurrection, while at the same time distancing such a celebration from the Christian holiday of Easter.

A third interpretation, which is still practiced today among Ethiopian Jews,[29] considers the "day after the shabbat" to be the 22nd day of the first month—the day after the *last* day of the Feast of *Matzah*. Similar to the traditional view, this interpretation may consider the *last* day of the Feast—a no-regular-work day—to be a Shabbat. Hence, the following day would be seen as the time to begin the counting.

Given the sequence and narrative of *Vayik'ra* 23, our opinion is that the timing derived from this third interpretation makes the most sense—though not necessarily for the reason cited. The other interpretations cause the counting from the *omer* and the days of the Feast of *Matzah* to overlap. It seems inconsistent with the rest of the calendar that *this* part would be so "messy." Rather, a simple, unbiased reading of *Vayik'ra* 23 tends to suggest a distinct sequence of events.

Since the entire controversy centers on the meaning of the Hebrew word שַׁבָּת, shabbat, let's investigate this a bit further. In *Vayik'ra* 23:15-16, שַׁבָּת, shabbat is used twice, as well as once in its plural form. We know that the word שַׁבָּת, shabbat does not always mean *a day of rest*.[30] We also know that this period of counting is to last for seven *weeks*[31]—in fact, the end of the counting culminates in *Shavuot*, which literally *means* "weeks." Given these facts, it is within the realm of possibility that *Vayik'ra* 23:15-16 can be translated,

> "And you will count from the day after the week (שַׁבָּת, shabbat), from the day of your bringing in the עֹמֶר, omer of the wave-offering,

---

[29] Beta Israel, or Falasha
[30] See *Vayik'ra* 25, which refers to every seventh year as a "shabbat."
[31] *D'variym* 16:9

there will be seven complete weeks (שַׁבָּתוֹת,
shabatot);[32] *count fifty days until the day after the*
seventh week (שַׁבָּת, shabbat),[33] *and you will bring*
near a new offering to ADONAI..."

If this interpretation can be accepted, then the "day after the shabbat" could very well be referring to the "day after the *week*" of the Feast of *Matzah*.[34] The counting period would then include seven full *weeks*—or 49 days. Practically speaking, this reckoning would have the same effect as that of the Ethiopian Jewish reckoning—the counting would begin on the 22nd day of the first month.[35]

Though this may seem like a *"foolish controversy... and dispute about the Law,"*[36] its importance lies in the fact that this time of counting affects the date of the next *moed*, *Shavuot*.[37] Though our personal view favors beginning the counting on the 22nd day of the first month—making a seamless transition from the week of the Feast of *Matzah*—we have chosen not to be

---

[32] Both the NIV and RSV, as well as the JPS Tanakh, translate the plural form of *shabbat* as "weeks" in this instance. The Septuagint, a Greek translation of the Hebrew Scriptures dating back to the first century BCE, also uses a word for "weeks."

[33] The JPS Tanakh and the Septuagint translate this occurrence of "shabbat"—the exact same word used in verse 15—as "week."

[34] The root meaning of שַׁבָּת, *shabbat* is "to cease" or "stop." In a sense, the Week of *Matzah* may be considered a "shabbat," in that it is also a time to *cease* from eating anything made with leaven.

[35] There are additional Scriptural factors that lead us to favor this timing, but further discussion is beyond the scope of this appendix.

[36] Titus 3:9

[37] If you are a member of a congregation that observes the *Mo'adiym*, we strongly encourage you to participate in your congregation's *Shavuot* celebration, regardless of when it falls. If your understanding of the counting period differs from that of your congregation, feel free to celebrate *Shavuot* on your own as well. We exhort you, however, to not allow any difference of opinion on this point to cause division within the community.

dogmatic about it with regard to the devotionals. This book simply contains seven devotionals for the Feast of *Matzah* and 49 for the counting period—and you may read them all, skip some, or double them up according to whatever reckoning you choose.

Feast of Weeks

The fiftieth day; the day after the seven weeks of counting
וַיִּקְרָא *Vayik'ra* 23:16b-22

The season of Spring *Mo'adiym* concludes with the one-day חַג הַשָּׁבֻעֹת, *Chag haShavuot*—the Feast of Weeks.[38] *Shavuot* occurs sometime during the beginning of the third month[39] when we have finished the counting from the *omer*.

Also called חַג הַקָּצִיר, *Chag haKatziyr* (Feast of the Harvest)[40] and יוֹם הַבִּכּוּרִים, *Yom haBikuriym* (Day of the First Fruits),[41] the primary feature of *Shavuot* is the first fruits offering from the newly matured wheat crops. Like the first and last days of the Feast of *Matzah*, *Shavuot* is a holy convocation and a no-regular-work day—again, rest is not commanded.

It is fascinating that there is no record in the Hebrew Scriptures of a significant event in Israel's history occurring on this day.[42] Indeed, the only

---

[38] Christianity refers to this day as "Pentecost," from the Greek word for "fiftieth."

[39] Depending on how the counting from the omer is reckoned, *Shavuot* could occur on any day between the 5th and 13th days of the third month.

[40] *Sh'mot* 23:16

[41] *B'mid'bar* 28:26

[42] Judaism associates the giving of the Torah at Sinai with *Shavuot*. This is because, according to *Sh'mot* 19, the Torah was given on the third day of the third month. Yet, Judaism fixes the date of *Shavuot* on the *sixth* day of the third month. So, while there is

Scriptural event directly linked to this *moed* is the giving of the Spirit as recounted in Acts 2.

The devotional for *Shavuot* is intended to be read on the day after the forty-nine days of the counting from the *omer*—the fiftieth day. Spiritual themes for this day may be related to the previous season of counting, including completion of growth, maturity, and fruitfulness. The events of Acts 2 are also obviously related, including the empowering fire of the Holy Spirit, and the bold proclamation the Good News of Yeshua.

"Feast of Trumpets"[43]

7ᵗʰ Month—1ˢᵗ Day (1 day)
וַיִּקְרָא *Vayik'ra* 23:23-25

In this passage, ADONAI commands:

> "*In the seventh month, on the first [day] of the month, have a rest,*[44] *a* זִכְרוֹן תְּרוּעָה, *zik'ron t'ruah, a holy convocation. Do no regular work...*"

There are few facts that we can clearly discern from this terse command. First, we know that this *moed* falls on the new moon, so we can infer that it shares some characteristics with the other eleven to twelve new moons that occur each calendar year.[45] Second, like

---

clearly a seasonal link between the *moed* and the giving of the Torah, there is no link to the actual day itself.
[43] "Feast of Trumpets" is the common nomenclature for this *moed* despite the fact that it is not a Feast, and is only linked with trumpets (*shofars* or ram's horns) by inference.
[44] שַׁבָּתוֹן, *shabaton*
[45] The new moon determines the beginning of each month on Israel's calendar. While not listed as a *moed* in *Vayik'ra* 23, there are specific sacrifices commanded for each new moon, and the silver trumpets are to be blown (*B'mid'bar* 10:10). Elsewhere in

many of the other *Mo'adiym*, this *moed* is a holy convocation or sacred assembly. Third, "rest" is specifically commanded on this day, unlike the previous no-regular-work days. As such, the level of activity for this *moed* is at least a degree more restful than the holy convocations of the Spring *Mo'adiym*.

But the unique feature of this *moed* is wrapped up in the phrase זִכְרוֹן תְּרוּעָה, *zik'ron t'ruah*. Unfortunately, the immediate context offers no help in clearly understanding its meaning.

In the most literal sense, and given the other occurrences of these words throughout Scripture, the phrase can be rendered, "remembrance (זִכְרוֹן, *zik'ron*) [with] loud blasts [of sound] (תְּרוּעָה, *t'ruah*)." In other words, we are supposed to remember or memorialize something, and this is either to be caused by or done in conjunction with loud blasts of sound. תְּהִלִּם, *T'hillim* (Psalms) 81:3 may offer us *some* insight into this mystery. It says,

> "Blow[46] a שׁוֹפָר, shofar in the חֹדֶשׁ, chodesh
> (new moon), [and] in the כֶּסֶה, keseh (full moon)
> at the day of our Feast..."

In this verse, we see a new moon, followed by a full moon that is also a Feast. There are only two possible months on Israel's calendar in which this pattern occurs—the first month, and seventh month.[47] However, the Scriptures assign no special significance to

---

Scripture, the new moon is often linked with Shabbat, indicating some level of spiritual significance to these days. See 2Kings 4:23 and Ezekiel 46:1. Themes of the new moon may include renewal, praise and worship.

[46] תָּקַע, *taka*

[47] The Feast at full moon during the first month is the Feast of *Matzah*. The Feast at full moon during the seventh month is *Sukot*.

the new moon of the first month, as it does to the new moon we are presently discussing. If this verse is indeed referring to the *moed* on the new moon of the seventh month, we may deduce that the *t'ruah* can be made through the blowing of the *shofar*.

In at least one other instance, there is a Scriptural connection between *t'ruah* and the *shofar*, but it is only by association. יְהוֹשֻׁעַ, Y'hoshua (Joshua) 6:20 recounts the collapse of the wall of Jericho. It says in part,

> "*And the people shouted (*רוּעַ, *rua), and blew (*תָּקַע, *taka) with the* שֹׁפָרוֹת, *shofarot, and it came to pass when the people heard the voice of the* שׁוֹפָר, *shofar, that the people shouted (*רוּעַ, *rua) [with] a great shout (*תְּרוּעָה גְדוֹלָה, *t'ruah g'dolah), and the wall fell flat...*"

In this passage, while the *shofar* is present, *it is not* what is making the *t'ruah*—the *people* are! Both here and in many other Scripture passages, *t'ruah* is the sound of people shouting, yelling or otherwise making loud sounds with their mouths.

Elsewhere in Scripture, *t'ruah* is the sound of alarm from the silver trumpets,[48] the sound of the *shofar* on *Yom haKipuriym* in the year of Jubilee,[49] a shout of praise,[50] a shout of joy,[51] and the playing of musical instruments[52]—in other words, "loud blasts [of sound]." But what does all this mean for the *moed* at hand? Here is a suggestion:

---

[48] *B'mid'bar* 10:5
[49] *Vayik'ra* 25:9
[50] 1Samuel 4:5-6, Ezra 3:11ff
[51] Job 8:21, Psalms 89:15
[52] Psalms 150:5

When we consider *t'ruah* in conjunction with the command for *zik'ron* (remembrance), maybe there is something that has to be jolted back to our minds by the surprising sounds of *t'ruah*—something we need to remember after the long, hot summer.[53] Indeed, this *moed* of *zik'ron t'ruah* opens a season of appointed times memorializing the great and wonderful provision, protection, atonement and deliverance of ADONAI— things we are constantly prone to forget. Perhaps we are to open our mouths with shouts of joy and make sounds of praise with our musical instruments in celebration of our great God, and in remembrance of His goodness, faithfulness and loving-kindness.

The devotional for the *moed* of *zik'ron t'ruah* is intended to be read on the first day of the seventh month with these themes in mind. While this understanding and approach to the *moed* is far removed from the traditional practice,[54] entering fully into the *moed* in such a way will surely make *zik'ron t'ruah* a day to remember!

---

[53] Following *Shavuot* in the third month, there are no *mo'adiym* until the first day of the seventh month.

[54] Despite the terse nature of the commands for this *moed*, the Judaisms have made it into *the* High Holy Day, second only to *Yom Kippur*. The lore surrounding the holiday is abundant, and the observance is extremely solemn. Traditionally, this *moed* is known as *Rosh Hashanah*, which literally means "Head of the Year." As mentioned earlier, Judaism recognizes the first day of the seventh month as the beginning of the new year. One of the main features of *Rosh Hashanah* is the blowing of the *shofar*, which, according to Judaism, fulfills the command to make *t'ruah*. Because Judaism so closely links this *moed* with the *shofar*, some Messianics and Christians have in turn connected this *moed* to prophetic Scriptures dealing with the Day of the Lord. But since the *moed* has no direct Scriptural link to the *shofar*, there is no solid ground for making such a prophetic leap. As believers in Yeshua, however, we have plenty to celebrate and remember on this *moed* without searching for additional meaning.

Day of the Atonements[55]
7th Month—10th Day (1 day)
וַיִּקְרָא *Vayik'ra* 23:26-32

יוֹם הַכִּפֻּרִים, *Yom haKipuriym* (Day of the Atonements) is arguably the holiest day on Israel's calendar, perhaps even surpassing the seventh-day Shabbat. Like the seventh day, *Yom haKipuriym* is a שַׁבַּת שַׁבָּתוֹן, *shabbat shabaton*[56]—a day to stop from all kinds of work and to rest completely. However, this day occurs only once each year, on the tenth day of the seventh month, with its observance beginning the evening before.

Far from being a feast, the primary feature of this holy convocation is to *deny oneself* or *afflict one's soul*. As the high priest[57] performs the atonements for himself, the altar, the tabernacle, and the whole community of Israel, the people participate through their non-participation. Not only are the people not allowed to come near the holy place on this day, but we are to deny our own existence. We are to stop *being* on this day by not even permitting ourselves the basic elements of survival—for instance, food and water.

But like *Pesach*, *Yom haKipuriym* finds its clear fulfillment in our Master, the Messiah Yeshua. As both our high priest and our sacrifice, He atoned for us once and for all, and is continually making intercession for us before the Father.[58] He does not need to make sacrifices for Himself and for us year after year in order to atone for our sins—it has already been accomplished forever.

---

[55] Traditionally, *Yom Kippur*—"Day of Atonement"
[56] *Yom haKipuriym* and the seventh day are the only *mo'adiym* that are also "shabbats."
[57] הַכֹּהֵן הַגָּדוֹל, *haCohen haGadol*
[58] Hebrews 7

Our self-denial on this day, therefore, does not cause, aid or enhance our atonement, but allows us to become acutely aware of our own mortality, our sin, our need for atonement, and our desire for life. At the same time, it causes us to appreciate on some minute level the sacrifice the Master made as He denied His own life on our behalf.

The sanctity and holiness of this day cannot be overstated. Though we may find great joy in our eternal atonement in the Messiah Yeshua, this is a day for remembering that atonement in such a way that will be very hard to forget. We are to be contemplative, repentant, humble, and dead to ourselves. On *Yom haKipuriym*, we are to remember that we live and breathe only because the Father so chooses—and that by His choice, He has the power to take it away as well.

As we read the devotional for *Yom haKipuriym* during the tenth day of the seventh month, these are the themes that we are to keep in mind—that without the Lord, we are truly dead; but that through Messiah's atoning blood and intercession, we are truly, truly alive!

Feast of Tabernacles

7ᵗʰ Month—15ᵗʰ Day through 21ˢᵗ Day (7 days)
וַיִּקְרָא *Vayik'ra* 23:33-36a, 39a, 40-43

The last great feast of Israel's annual calendar is חַג הַסֻּכּוֹת, *Chag haSukot* (Feast of the Tabernacles). It is also called חַג הָאָסִף, *Chag haAsif* (Feast of the Ingathering), because it occurs at *"the outgoing of the year, when you gather in [the fruit of] your labor from the field."*[59]

---

[59] *Sh'mot* 23:16

Like the Feast of *Matzah, Sukot* lasts seven days and is a time for great celebration. But unlike the Feast of *Matzah,* only the *first* day of *Sukot* is a holy convocation.[60] On this day, Israel is commanded to do no regular work, and to rest. *Sukot* begins just five days after *Yom HaKipuriym* on the fifteenth day of the seventh month, and lasts until the twenty-first day.

The primary feature of *Sukot* is, of course, the סֻכָּה, *sukah*—a.k.a. "booth" or "tabernacle"—which is to be constructed from the various trees and flora surrounding Jerusalem.[61] The purpose of the *sukah* is to remind us that ADONAI caused the people of Israel to live in *sukot* when He brought them out of Egypt. From this, we can draw out the spiritual themes of divine protection, deliverance, and provision. The impermanent and flimsy nature of the *sukah* itself should also remind us of our own weakness, fragility, and impermanence—as long as we dwell in our earthly bodies. The *sukah* is a symbol of how ADONAI cares for us, shades and hides us from the elements bent on our destruction. At the time of the final ingathering, we are to celebrate with extreme joy that He delivered us, watched over us, and will soon be taking us to dwell with Him in the *sukah* that will last forever.

In order to get the most out of the *Sukot* devotionals, it is recommended that they be read while sitting—and, if possible, actually living—in a *sukah.* Words cannot describe the experience of *Sukot,* and an element of the devotionals may be lost in an alternative environment. If a *sukah* is not an option for you at this

---

[60] In Judaism, the seventh day of *Sukot* came to be known as *Hoshanna Rabba,* and was celebrated with a huge water libation ceremony to plead for abundant rain over the next season.
[61] See *Vayik'ra* 23:40 as well as *N'chem'yah* 8:14ff

time, anyplace outdoors—perhaps under a tree, or in a gazebo—will aid in your devotional experience.

The seven devotionals for *Sukot* are intended to be read on the fifteenth through the twenty-first days of the seventh month.

Eighth Day Assembly

7ᵗʰ Month—22ⁿᵈ Day (1 day)
וַיִּקְרָא *Vayik'ra* 23:36b, 39c

Immediately following the seven-day Feast of *Sukot* is the closing *moed* of the year—יוֹם הַשְּׁמִינִי עֲצֶרֶת, *Yom haSh'miyniy 'Atzaret*[62] (The Eighth Day Assembly). The commands for this day are very simple: do no regular work, rest—and assemble.[63]

In short, the Eighth Day is a time to say "good-bye" to *Sukot* and the past year's *mo'adiym*. It's a time to rest and reflect, but also a time to look forward to the future—because in just six short months, it all starts over again.

Though this *moed* is often tossed aside as being insignificant,[64] it can be an extremely meaningful time—if we will let it. **The devotional for the twenty-second day of the seventh month wraps up the entire book** by encouraging us to look back at the journey we will have finally finished, but also to look forward to the incredible times that lay ahead.

---

[62] *B'mid'bar 29:35*
[63] Different kinds of animal sacrifices are commanded for this as well as all the other *mo'adiym* (with the exception of the days of counting from the *omer*).
[64] Or instead celebrated as *Simchat Torah*, an extra-biblical Jewish holiday.

The Mo'adiym—Discipleship By Design

The *Mo'adiym* are so much more than times to practice our ritual Jewishness, or days to ponder prophetically without actual participation. The *Mo'adiym* offer us a unique opportunity for being discipled by the Spirit, as we walk in the ways of the Son, toward our full potential and usefulness for the Father. As we devote ourselves to living out the fullness of the *Mo'adiym*, those of us who are Jewish will more fully understand our calling as the people of Israel—and *all* of us as believers in Messiah will draw closer to Him, becoming more effective, powerful, and victorious disciples for Yeshua.

The *Messianic Mo'adiym Devotional* is a tool for helping you get the most out of each *moed* on Israel's annual calendar. As you walk through the *Mo'adiym* every year, allow the Spirit to sow in you the deep truths that each *moed* is designed to help you remember, so that the Father may gather in a great harvest through you—for the glory of His great name, and for the name of His Son... our Master and King, the Messiah Yeshua.

Annual Mo'adiym Calendar

Moed	Theme	Month	Day	
SPRING				
Pesach	Freedom		14	at sundown
Feast of Matzah (7 days)	Walking out our reality in Messiah of being "unleavened"	1	15 16 17 18 19 20 21 22	Possible alternative dates for starting the count from the omer.
Counting from the Omer (49 days)	Growing toward maturity	2	↑ ↓ 4	
Shavuot (1 day)	Fire, fruitfulness, harvest	3	5 6 7 8 9 10 11 12 13	Range of possible dates for Shavuot—depends on omer.
FALL				
T'ruah	Remembrance		1	
Yom haKipuriym	Atonement		10	
Sukot (7 days)	Abiding in ADONAI's protection and provision	7	15 16 17 18 19 20 21	
Yom haSh'miyniy	Reflection		22	

About the Author

Kevin Geoffrey, born Kevin Geoffrey Berger, is the firstborn son of a first-generation American, non-religious, secular Jewish family. Ashamed of his heritage from childhood, Kevin deliberately attempted to hide his identity as a Jew. He spent his youth like most Jewish kids—essentially assimilated into American culture, embracing the things of the world and pursuing the things of the flesh.

At fifteen years of age, Kevin was diagnosed with Crohn's disease, a serious and incurable disorder of the digestive tract. After experiencing a sudden and apparently miraculous healing, Kevin's heart was opened to consider the possibility of something in which he had always been taught not to believe: the existence of God. A few years later, through various influential encounters and relationships, Kevin accepted Yeshua as Messiah and became what he then understood as a "born-again Christian."

Upon graduating from high school, Kevin rejected higher learning to half-heartedly pursue a career in music. With delusions of grandeur and his newfound identity as a "Christian," Kevin legally changed his name to Kevin Geoffrey, completing his assimilation from "Jew" to "Christian." When his ambition as a "rock star" ultimately failed to materialize, Kevin conceded defeat and entered Jacksonville University (Florida), where he graduated *magna cum laude*.

Throughout college, Kevin zealously studied the Scriptures. Seeking like-minded believers, he visited several Christian churches, but he was unable to find a place to call home. It was during this time that Kevin revealed his Jewish heritage to a close friend, who introduced him to the existence of the Messianic Jewish Movement.

In 1996, shortly before meeting his soon-to-be wife Esther, Kevin became part of a non-denominational Christian Fellowship where he was discipled in his faith, as well as in praise and worship ministry. Together, Kevin and Esther continued to learn about the Messianic Jewish Movement and became occasional attendees at the local Messianic congregation. Finally, after their Christian Fellowship suffered a devastating split, Kevin was able to fully embrace his call as a Messianic Jew and was restored to his Jewish heritage.

Today, Kevin is a strong advocate for the restoration of Jewish believers in Yeshua to their distinct calling and identity as the remnant of Israel. Kevin is the founder of Perfect Word Ministries, a Messianic Jewish equipping ministry, which he currently serves as President and Director. He is the author of the *Messianic Devotional* and *The Messianic Life* series, and is a regular contributor to *Jewish Voice Today* magazine. In 2006, Kevin was licensed as a Messianic Jewish Teacher by the International Alliance of Messianic Congregations and Synagogues, and by Jewish Voice Ministries International. Kevin has taught in live seminars and conferences throughout the United States, as well as multiple Messianic congregations and synagogues. He has also served in congregational leadership, and as an anointed worship leader both in congregations and in regional and national Messianic conferences. Kevin resides in Phoenix, Arizona with his wife Esther and their three beautiful sons, Isaac, Josiah and Hosea.

PERFECT Word
M · I · N · I · S · T · R · I · E · S

A Messianic Jewish Equipping Ministry

Other Resources Available from Perfect Word

Monthly Teachings

- ❖ *The Messianic Life* discipleship publication
- ❖ *Preparing The Way* audio teachings

Devotional Books

- ❖ Messianic Daily Devotional
- ❖ Messianic Mo'adiym Devotional
- ❖ Messianic Torah Devotional (Fall 2007)

The Messianic Life Series
Small Group & Personal Study Resources

- ❖ Being A Disciple of Messiah
- ❖ The Fruit of the Spirit

www.PerfectWordMinistries.com

**Calling the Body of Messiah to maturity
by teaching the simple application of Scripture
for a radically changed life in Yeshua**

Printed in the United States
214172BV00001B/78/A

9 780978 550417